Mountains and Rivers Without End

Gary Snyder

Mountains

and *Rivers*

Without

End

COUNTERPOINT

WASHINGTON, D.C.

The author gratefully acknowledges permission to reprint previ-
ously published material. A publication record appears on page 165.

LIBRARY OF CONGRESS CATALOGING-IN-PUBLICATION DATA
Snyder, Gary, 1930–
    Mountains and rivers without end / Gary Snyder.
    Completed work appears for the 1st time in this volume.
    I. Title.
    PS3569.N88M62   1996
    811'.54—dc20   96–26064
                                                    CIP
    ISBN 1–887178–20–1 (hardcover : alk. paper).
    ISBN 1–887178–52–x (hardcover : limited ed. : alk. paper)

FIRST PRINTING

Printed in the United States of America on acid-free paper that meets
the American National Standards Institute z39–48 Standard

Endpapers: *Streams and Mountains Without End* (early twelfth cen-
tury), China, Northern Sung Dynasty, courtesy of The Cleveland
Museum of Art
Frontispiece: Detail from *Streams and Mountains Without End*
Drawing of Kokop'ele on page 79: Gary Snyder
Image of Tārā on page 112: Courtesy of Gary Snyder
Design and electronic production by David Bullen

COUNTERPOINT
P.O. Box 65793
Washington, D.C. 20035–5793

Distributed by Publishers Group West

This book is for

Gen,
Kai,
Mika,
Kyung-jin

Contents

The notion of Emptiness engenders Compassion.

Milarepa

An ancient Buddha said "A painted rice cake does not satisfy hunger." Dogen comments:

"There arc few who have even seen this 'painting of a rice cake' and none of them has thoroughly understood it.

"The paints for painting rice-cakes are the same as those used for painting mountains and waters.

"If you say the painting is not real, then the material phenomenal world is not real, the Dharma is not real.

"Unsurpassed enlightenment is a painting. The entire phenomenal universe and the empty sky are nothing but a painting.

"Since this is so, there is no remedy for satisfying hunger other than a painted rice cake. Without painted hunger you never become a true person."

Dōgen, "Painting of a Rice Cake"

Mountains and Rivers Without End

I

Endless Streams and Mountains
Ch'i Shan Wu Chin

Clearing the mind and sliding in
        to that created space,
a web of waters streaming over rocks,
air misty but not raining,
        seeing this land from a boat on a lake
        or a broad slow river,
        coasting by.

The path comes down along a lowland stream
slips behind boulders and leafy hardwoods,
reappears in a pine grove,

no farms around, just tidy cottages and shelters,
gateways, rest stops, roofed but unwalled work space,
        —a warm damp climate;

a trail of climbing stairsteps forks upstream.
Big ranges lurk behind these rugged little outcrops—
these spits of low ground rocky uplifts
        layered pinnacles aslant,
flurries of brushy cliffs receding,
far back and high above, vague peaks.
A man hunched over, sitting on a log
        another stands above him, lifts a staff,
a third, with a roll of mats or a lute, looks on;
a bit offshore two people in a boat.

The trail goes far inland,
        somewhere back around a bay,

lost in distant foothill slopes
        & back again
at a village on the beach, and someone's fishing.

Rider and walker cross a bridge
above a frothy braided torrent
that descends from a flurry of roofs like flowers
      temples tucked between cliffs,
          a side trail goes there;

a jumble of cliffs above,
ridge tops edged with bushes,
valley fog below a hazy canyon.

A man with a shoulder load leans into the grade.
Another horse and a hiker,
the trail goes up along cascading streambed
no bridge in sight—
comes back through chinquapin or
liquidambars; another group of travelers.
Trail's end at the edge of an inlet
below a heavy set of dark rock hills.
Two moored boats with basket roofing,
      a boatman in the bow looks
         lost in thought.

      Hills beyond rivers, willows in a swamp,
      a gentle valley reaching far inland.

      The watching boat has floated off the page.

    •

At the end of the painting the scroll continues on with seals and poems. It tells a further tale:

"—Wang Wen-wei saw this at the mayor's house in Ho-tung town, year 1205. Wrote at the end of it,

> 'The Fashioner of Things
>   has no original intentions
> Mountains and rivers
>   are spirit, condensed.'

> '. . . Who has come up with
>   these miraculous forests and springs?
> Pale ink
>   on fine white silk.'

Later that month someone named Li Hui added,

> '. . . Most people can get along with the noise of dogs
>   and chickens;
>   Everybody cheerful in these peaceful times.
>   But I—why are my tastes so odd?
>   I love the company of streams and boulders.'

T'ien Hsieh of Wei-lo, no date, next wrote,

> '. . . The water holds up the mountains,
>   The mountains go down in the water . . . '

In 1332 Chih-shun adds,

> '. . . This is truly a painting worth careful keeping.
>   And it has poem-colophons from the Sung and the

Chin dynasties. That it survived dangers of fire and
war makes it even rarer.'

In the mid-seventeenth century one Wang To had a look at it:

'My brother's relative by marriage, Wên-sun, is learned and
has good taste. He writes good prose and poetry. My broth-
er brought over this painting of his to show me . . . '

The great Ch'ing dynasty collector Liang Ch'ing-piao owned it,
but didn't write on it or cover it with seals. From him it went into
the Imperial collection down to the early twentieth century. Chang
Ta-ch'ien sold it in 1949. Now it's at the Cleveland Art Museum,
which sits on a rise that looks out toward the waters of Lake Erie.

•

Step back and gaze again at the land:
                    it rises and subsides —

ravines and cliffs like waves of blowing leaves —
          stamp the foot, walk with it, clap! turn,
          the creeks come in, ah!
          strained through boulders,
          mountains walking on the water,
          water ripples every hill.

—I walk out of the museum—low gray clouds over the lake—
chill March breeze.

•

Old ghost ranges, sunken rivers, come again
          stand by the wall and tell their tale,
walk the path, sit the rains,
grind the ink, wet the brush, unroll the
          broad white space:

lead out and tip
the moist black line.

Walking on walking,
                    under foot   earth turns.

Streams and mountains never stay the same.

Note: A hand scroll by this name showed up in Shansi province, central China, in the thirteenth century. Even then the painter was unknown, "a person of the Sung Dynasty." Now it's on Turtle Island. Unroll the scroll to the left, a section at a time, as you let the right side roll back in. Place by place unfurls.

Old Bones

Out there walking round, looking out for food,
a rootstock, a birdcall, a seed that you can crack
plucking, digging, snaring, snagging,
     barely getting by,

no food out there on dusty slopes of scree—
carry some—look for some,
go for a hungry dream.
Deer bone, Dall sheep,
     bones hunger home.

Out there somewhere
a shrine for the old ones,
the dust of the old bones,
     old songs and tales.

What we ate—who ate what—
     how we all prevailed.

Night Highway 99

Only the very poor, or eccentric, can surround themselves with shapes of elegance (soon to be demolished) in which they are forced by poverty to move with leisurely grace. We remain alert so as not to get run down, but it turns out you only have to hop a few feet to one side and the whole huge machinery rolls by, not seeing you at all.

Lew Welch

We're on our way

           man
       out of town
    go hitching down
   that highway 99

Too cold and rainy to go out on the Sound
Sitting in Ferndale drinking coffee
Baxter in black, been to a funeral
Raymond in Bellingham—Helena Hotel—
Can't go to Mexico with that weak heart
Well you boys can go south. I stay here.
Fix up a shack—get a part-time job—
       (he disappeared later
        maybe found in the river)
In Ferndale & Bellingham
Went out on trail crews
Glacier and Marblemount
There we part.

      Tiny men with mustaches
      driving ox teams
      deep in the cedar groves

                    wet brush, tin pants, snoose—

Split-shake roof barns
            over berry fields
                        white birch chicken coop

Put up in Dick Meigs cabin
            out behind the house—
Coffeecan, PA tin, rags, dirty cups,
Kindling fell behind the stove, miceshit,
            old magazines,

                        winter's coming in the mountains
                        shut down the show
                        the punks go back to school
                        and the rest hit the road—

            strawberries picked, shakeblanks split
            fires all out and the packstrings brought
            down to the valleys:
                        set loose to graze.

Gray wharves and hacksaw gothic homes
Shingle mills and stump farms

                                    overgrown.

            •

Fifty weary Indians   Mt. Vernon
Sleep in the bus station
Strawberry pickers speaking Kwakiutl
            turn at Burlington for Skagit & Ross Dam

under apple trees by the river
banks of junked cars

BC Riders give hitchhikers rides

"The sheriff's posse stood in double rows   Everett
        flogged the naked Wobblies down
        with stalks of Devil's Club
        & run them out of town"

While shingle weavers lost their fingers
        in the tricky feed and take
                of double saws.

Dried, shrimp   Seattle
        smoked, salmon
—before the war old Salish gentleman came
& sold us kids rich hard-smoked Chinook
from his flatbed model T
        Lake City,

        waste of trees & topsoil, beast, herb,
        edible roots, Indian field-farms & white men
        dances   washed, leached, burnt out
        minds blunt, ug! talk twisted

        a night of the long poem
        and the mined guitar
        "Forming the new society
        within the shell of the old"
                mess of tincan camps and littered roads.

The Highway passes straight through every town
    at Matsons washing bluejeans
        hills and saltwater

           ack, the woodsmoke in my brain

    (high Olympics — can't go there again)

East Marginal Way the hitchhike zone
Boeing down across Duwamish slough
and angle out   & on.

   •

Night rain wet concrete headlights blind   Tacoma

    salt air / bulk cargo / steam cycle / AIR REDUCTION

    eating peanuts I don't give a damn
    if anybody ever stops   I'll walk
    to San Francisco   what the hell

        "that's where you going?
        why you got that pack?"

        "well man I just don't feel right
        without something on my back"

           & this character in milkman overalls
           "I have to come out here
           every once in a while, there's a guy
           blows me here"

           way out of town.

Stayed in Olympia with Dick Meigs
      —this was a different year & he had moved—
      sleep on a cot in the back yard
      half the night watch shooting stars

These guys got babies now
      drink beer, come back from wars,
      "I'd like to save up all my money
      get a big new car, go down to Reno

      & latch onto one of those rich girls—
      I'd fix their little ass"—nineteen yr old
      North Dakota boy fixing to get married next month.

To Centralia in a purple Ford.

          Carstruck dead doe
          by the Skookumchuck river

Fat man in a Chevrolet
      wants to go back to L.A.   "too damned poor now"

Airbrakes on the log trucks hiss and whine
      stand in the dark by the stoplight
          big fat cars tool by
      drink coffee, drink more coffee
          brush teeth back of Shell

      hot shoes
          stay on the rightside of that
             yellow line

Mary's Corner, turn for Mt. Rainier
      —once caught a ride at night for Portland here.
Five Mexicans ask me "chip in on the gas."
      I never was more broke & down.

      Got fired that day by the USA
      (the District Ranger up at Packwood
      thought the Wobblies had been dead for
          forty years
      but the FBI smelled treason
          —my red beard)

That Waco Texas boy
      took A.G. and me through miles of snow
      had a chest of logger gear
      at the home of an Indian girl
      in Kelso hadn't seen since fifty-four

Toledo, Castle Rock, free way four lane
      no stoplights and no crossings, only cars,
      & people walking, old hitchhikers
      break the laws. How do I know . . .
          the state cop
            told me so.

    Come a dozen times into
          Portland
    on the bum or
        hasty lover
    late at night.

     •

Dust kicking up behind the trucks—night rides—
Who waits in the coffee stop
                    night highway 99

    Sokei-an met an old man on the banks of the
    Columbia growing potatoes & living all alone,
    Sokei-an asked him the reason why he lived there,
    he said

    Boy, no one ever asked me the reason why,
    I like to be alone.
    I am an old man.
    I have forgotten how to speak human words.

All night freezing in the back of a truck
    dawn at Smith River
    battering on in loggers' pickups
                prunes for lunch
The next night, Siuslaw.

Portland sawdust down town
Buttermilk corner all you want for a nickel
    (now a dime)   —Sujata gave
Gautama buttermilk.
(No doubt! says Sokei-an, that's all it was:
    plain buttermilk)

    rim of mountains,
    pulp bark chewed snag papermill
    tugboom in the river
    —used to lean on bridge rails
    dreaming up eruptions and quakes—

Slept under juniper in the Siskiyou   Yreka
        a sleeping bag, a foot of snow
        black rolled umbrella
        ice slick asphalt

Caught a ride the only car come by
        at seven in the morning
        chewing froze salami
        riding with a passed-out L.A. whore
        glove compartment full of booze,
        the driver a rider,
                nobody cowboy,
        sometime hood,
Like me picked up to drive,
        & drive the blues away.
                We drank to Portland
                        and we treated that girl good.
I split my last two bucks with him in town
        went out to Carol & Billy's in the woods.

                Foggy morning in Newport
                housetrailers
                        under the fir.

                •

An old book on Japan at the Goodwill
        unfurled umbrella in the sailing snow
                sat back in black wood
                        barber college
                chair, a shave

On Second Street in Portland.
                What elegance. What a life.
                Bust my belly with a quart of
                buttermilk
                & five dry heels of French bread
                from the market cheap
                                clean shaved, dry feet,

We're on our way
                man
                        out of town

Go hitching down that
                highway 99.

                •

Oil pump broken, motor burning out   Salem

Ex-logger selling skidder cable
        wants to get to San Francisco,
        fed and drunk   Eugene

Guy just back from Alaska—don't like
        the States now—too much law   Sutherlin

A woman with a kid & two bales of hay   Roseburg

Sawmill worker, young guy thinking of
        going to Eureka for redwood logging
        later in the year   Dillard

Two Assembly of God Pentecostal boys from
     a holy-roller high school. One had
        spoken in tongues   Canyonville

     (LASME Lost Angeles–Seattle Motor Express)
        place on highway 20
        LITTLE ELK
        badger & badger

South of Yoncalla burn the engine
     run out of oil (a different car)
(Six great highways; so far only one)

Jumpoff Joe Creek &
     a man carrying nothing, walking sort of
     stiff-legged along, blue jeans & denim jacket
     wrinkled face, just north of
     Louse Creek

        —Abandon really means it
        the network womb stretched loose all
           things slip through

     Dreaming on a bench under newspapers
     I woke covered with rhododendron blooms
        alone in a State Park in Oregon.

        •

     "I had a girl in Oakland who worked
     for a doctor, she was a nurse, she let him
     eat her. She died of tuberculosis

& I drove back that night to Portland
nonstop, crying all the way"   Grants Pass

"I picked up a young mother with two
children once, their house had just burned down"

"I picked up an Italian tree-surgeon
in Port Angeles once, he had all his
saws and tools all screwed & bolted on
        a beat-up bike."

Oxyoke, Wolf Creek, a guy
Coming off a five-day binge to   Phoenix
An ex-bartender from Lebanon to   Redding
Man & wife on a drinking spree, to   Anderson

Snow on the pines & firs around Lake Shasta
        —Chinese scene of winter hills and trees
        us "little travelers" in the bitter cold
        six-lane highway slash & D—9 Cats—
        bridge building   squat earth-movers
        —yellow bugs
                        I speak for hawks. Creating
        "Shasta" as I go—

The road that's followed goes forever;
        in half a minute crossed and left behind.

Out of the snow and into red-dirt plains
        blossoming plums

Each time you go that road it gets more straight
        curves across the mountain lost in fill

towns you had to slow down all four lane
      Azalea, Myrtle Creek

watch out for deer.

At Project City Indian hitcher
Standing under single tarpole lamp
    nobody stopped
        we walked four miles
        to an oak fire left by the road crew,
          shivered the night away.

      •

Going to San Francisco
Yeah San Francisco
Yeah we came from Seattle
Even farther north
Yeah we been working in the mountains
    in the spring
    in the autumn
        I always go this highway 99—

    "I was working in a mill three weeks there
    then it burned down & the guy didn't even
    pay us off—but I can do anything—
    I'll go to San Francisco—tend bar—"

Sixteen speeds forward   windows open
Stopped at the edge of Willows for a bite
      grass shoots on the edge of
      drained rice plains
        —where are the Sierras—

•

standing in the night   in the world-end winds
by the overpass bridge
      junction US 40   and highway 99

      trucks, trucks,   roll by
      kicking up dust   dead flowers

      level, dry,
Highway turns west.
        Miles gone, speed still
        pass through lower hills
        heat drying
        toward Vallejo
        gray on the salt baywater
           brown grass ridges
              buckbrush blue.

Herons in the tideflats
      have no thought for
States of Cars

      —I'm sick of car exhaust

        City
      gleaming far away
we make it into town tonight
get clean and drink some wine—

       SAN FRANCISCO

        NO
       body

gives a shit
man
who you are
or what's your car
there
IS no   99

Three Worlds, Three Realms, Six Roads

Things to Do Around Seattle

Hear phone poles hum
Catch garter snakes. Make lizard tails fall off;
Biking to Lake Washington, catch muddy little fish.
Peeling old bark off madrone to see the clean red new bark
Cleaning fir pitch off your hands
Reading books in the back of the University District Goodwill.
Swim in Puget Sound below the railroad tracks
Dig clams
Ride the Kalakala to Bremerton
See Mt. Constance from the water tower up by the art museum
Fudgsicles in Woodland Park zoo, the eagle and the camel
The mummy Eskimo baby in the University Anthropology
          museum.
Hung up deep sea canoes, red cedar log.
Eating old-style oatmeal mush cooked in a double boiler
          or cracked-wheat cereal with dates.
Sway in the wind in the top of the cedar in the middle of the
          swamp
Walk through the swamp and over the ridge to the pine woods,
Picking wild blackberries all around the stumps.
Peeling cascara
Feeding chickens
Feeling Penelope's udder, one teat small.
Oregon grape and salal.

Things to Do Around Portland

Go walk along the Sandy when the smelt run
Drink buttermilk at the Buttermilk Corner
Walk over Hawthorne Bridge the car tires sing

Take the trolley out to Sellwood when cherries are in bloom
Hiking the woods below Council Crest, a tree house high in a
      Douglas fir near the medical school.
Bird watching and plant hunting on Sauvies Island in May
Vine maple leaves in the slopes above St. John's Bridge in autumn
Wading the Columbia out to sandbars
Himalayan blackberries tangle at the base of steel high-tension
      Bonneville transmission tower—your fingers stained
Get married in Vancouver without the three-day wait.
Cash paychecks at the Pastime
Beer in Ericson's, hamburgers at Tic Tock.
Led down narrow corridors of Court House, City Hall, the
      newspapers, the radios, the jail.
Parking in the Park blocks
Sunburned skiing
Shivering at the ocean
Standing in the rain

Things to Do Around a Lookout

Wrap up in a blanket in cold weather and just read.
Practice writing Chinese characters with a brush
Paint pictures of the mountains
Put out salt for deer
Bake coffee cake and biscuit in the iron oven
Hours off hunting twisty firewood, packing it all back up and
      chopping.
Rice out for the ptarmigan and the conies
Mark well sunrise and sunset—drink lapsang soochong.
Rolling smokes
The flower book and the bird book and the star book
Old Reader's Digests left behind
Bullshitting on the radio with a distant pinnacle like you hid in
      clouds

Drawing little sexy sketches of bare girls
Reading maps, checking on the weather, airing out musty Forest
Service sleeping bags and blankets
Oil the saws, sharpen axes,
Learn the names of all the peaks you see and which is highest—
there are hundreds—
Learn by heart the drainages between
Go find a shallow pool of snowmelt on a good day, bathe in the
lukewarm water
Take off in foggy weather and go climbing all alone
The rock book—strata, dip, and strike
Get ready for the snow, get ready
To go down.

Things to Do Around San Francisco

Catch eels in the rocks below the Palace of the Legion of Honor.
Four in the morning—congee at Sam Wo.
Walk up and down Market, upstairs playing pool,
Turn on at Aquatic park—seagulls steal bait sardine
Going clear out to Oh's to buy bulghur.
Howard Street Goodwill
Not paying traffic tickets; stopping the phone.
Merry-go-round at the beach, the walk up to the cliff house,
sea lions and tourists—the old washed-out road that goes
on—
Play chess at Mechanics'
Dress up and go looking for work
Seek out the Wu-t'ung trees in the park arboretum.
Suck in the sea air and hold it—miles of white walls—
sunset shoots back from somebody's window high in the
Piedmont hills
Get drunk all the time. Go someplace and score.
Walk in and walk out of the Asp

Hike up Tam
Keep quitting and starting at Berkeley
Watch the pike in the Steinhart Aquarium: he doesn't move.
Sleeping with strangers
Keeping up on the news
Chanting sutras after sitting
Practicing yr frailing on guitar
Get dropped off in the fog in the night
Fall in love twenty times
Get divorced
Keep moving—move out to the Sunset
Get lost—or
Get found

Things to Do Around a Ship at Sea

Go out with a small flashlight and a star chart on a clear night
	and check out the full size of Eridanus.
Sunbathe on a cot on the boatdeck
Go forward and talk with the lookout, away from the engines, the
	silence and shudder
Watch running lights pass in the night.
Dolphins and sharks.
Phosphorescing creatures alongside the shipside, burning spots in
	the wake.
Stag, Argosy, Playboy, and Time.
Do pushups.
Make coffee in the galley, telling jokes.
Type letters to his girlfriend in Naples for the twelve-to-four
	Oiler
Sew up jeans.
Practise tying knots and whipping
Watch the Chief Cook singing blues
Tell big story lies

Grow a beard
Learn to weld and run a lathe
Study for the Firemans Oilers and Watertenders exam
Tropic- and sea-bird watching
Types of ships
Listening to hours of words and lifetimes—fuck and shit—
Figuring out the revolution
Hammer pipes and flanges
Paint a picture on a bulkhead with leftover paints
Dream of girls, about yr girlfriend, writing letters, wanting
    children,
Making plans

Things to Do Around Kyoto

Lie on the mats and sweat in summer,
Shiver in winter, sit and soak like a foetus in the bath.
Paikaru and gyoza at Min Min with Marxist students full of
    China
Look for country pothooks at the Nijo junk store
Get dry bad red wine to drink like a regular foreigner, from
    Maki's
Trudging around with visitors to gardens

Pluck weeds out of the moss. Plant morning glories
Walk down back alleys listening to looms
Watching the flocks of sparrows whirling over trees on winter
    sunsets
Get up at four in the morning to go meet with the Old Man.
Sitting in deep samadhi on a hurting knee.
Get buttered up by bar girls, pay too much
Motorcycle oil change down on Gojo
Warm up your chilly wife, her big old feet.

Trying to get a key made
Trying to find brown bread
Hunting rooms for Americans
Having a big meeting, speaking several tongues.

Lose your way in the bamboo brush on Hiei-zan in winter
Step on a bug by mistake
Quiet weeks and weeks, walking and reading, talking and
     weeding
Passing the hand around a rough cool pot
Throwing away the things you'll never need
Stripping down
Going home.

Jackrabbit

Jackrabbit,
black-tailed Hare
by the side of the road,
hop, stop.

Great ears shining,
you know me
a little. A lot more than I
know you.

The Elwha River

I was a girl waiting by the roadside for my boyfriend to come in his car. I was pregnant. I should have been going to high school. I walked up the road when he didn't come, over a bridge: I saw a sleeping man. I came to the Elwha River—the grade school— classes—I went and sat down with the children. The teacher was young and sad-looking, homely; she assigned us an essay: "What I Just Did." I wrote,

> "I was waiting for my boyfriend by the Elwha River bridge: the bridge was redwood, a fresh bridge with inner bark still clinging on some logs—it smelled good. There was some- one sleeping under redwood trees. He had a box of flies by his head and he was on the ground. The Elwha River bridge is by a meadow; there's a rocky bar there where the river forks . . ."

thinking this would please the teacher. We handed all the papers in, and got them back—mine was C minus. The children then went home. The teacher came to me and said "I just don't like you." —"Why?"
—"Because I used to be a man."

The Elwha River, I explained, is a real river, and different from the river I described. Where I had just walked was real, but I wrote a dream river—actually the Elwha doesn't fork at that point.

> As I write this now I must remind myself that there is another Elwha, the actual Olympic peninsula river, which is not the river I took pains to recollect as real in the dream.

> There are no redwoods north of southern
>   Curry County, Oregon.

Bubbs Creek Haircut

High ceilinged and the double mirrors, the
        calendar a splendid alpine scene—scab barber—
in stained white barber gown, alone, sat down, old man
a summer fog gray San Francisco day
I walked right in. On Howard Street
                haircut a dollar twenty-five.
Just clip it close as it will go.
        "Now why you want your hair cut back like that."
        —Well I'm going to the Sierras for a while
Bubbs Creek and on across to upper Kern.
        He wriggled clippers
"Well I been up there, I built the cabin
        up at Cedar Grove. In nineteen five."
            Old haircut smell.

Next door, Goodwill
        where I came out.
A search for sweater and a stroll
        in the board & concrete room of
        unfixed junk downstairs—
all emblems of the past—too close—
        heaped up in chilly dust and bare-bulb glare
of tables, wheelchairs, battered trunks & lamps
& pots that boiled up coffee nineteen ten, things
swimming on their own & finally freed
        from human need. Or?
      Waiting a final flicker of desire
to tote them out once more. Some freakish use.
The Master of the limbo drag-legged watches
        making prices
      to the people seldom buy.
The sag-asst rocker has to make it now. Alone.

A few days later drove with Locke
down San Joaquin, us barefoot in the heat
stopping for beer and melon on the way
                    the Giant Orange,
rubber shreds of cast truck retreads on the pebble
shoulder, highway 99.
                    Sierras marked by cumulus in the east.
Car coughing in the groves,   six thousand feet
down to Kings River Canyon; camped at Cedar Grove.
          Hard granite canyon walls that
          leave no scree.

Once tried a haircut at the Barber College too—
sat half an hour before they told me
                    white men use the other side.
Goodwill, St. Vincent de Paul,
                    Salvation Army up the coast
for mackinaws and boots and heavy socks
          —Seattle has the best for logger gear
once found a pair of good tricouni boots
                    at the under-the-public market store,
                    Mark Tobey's scene,
                              torn down I hear—
and Filson jacket with a birdblood stain.

A.G. and me got winter clothes for almost nothing
          at Lake Union, telling the old gal
          we was on our way
to work the winter out up in B.C.
                    hitchhiking home the
green hat got a ride (of that more later).

Hiking up Bubbs Creek saw the trail crew tent
in a scraggly grove of creekside lodgepole pine
            talked to the guy, he says

"If you see McCool on the other trail crew over there
tell him Moorehead says to go to hell."
Late snow that summer. Crossing the scarred bare
            shed of Forester Pass
      the winding rock-braced switchbacks
dive in snowbanks, we climb on where
            pack trains have to dig or wait.
A half-iced-over lake, twelve thousand feet
            its sterile boulder bank
but filled with leaping trout:
            reflections wobble in the
mingling circles always spreading out
      the crazy web of wavelets makes sense
      seen from high above.
A deva world of sorts—it's high
            —a view that few men see, a point
      bare sunlight
      on the spaces
empty sky
            molding to fit the shape of what ice left
of fire-thrust, or of tilted, twisted, faulted
                  cast-out from this lava belly globe.

The boulder in my mind's eye is a chair.
                  . . . why was the man drag-legged?
King of Hell
      or is it a paradise of sorts, thus freed
from acting out the function some

creator / carpenter
thrust on a thing to think he made, himself,
an object always "chair" ?
Sinister ritual histories.
Is the Mountain God a gimp?
The halting metrics   and the ritual limp,
Good   Will?

Daughter of mountains, stooped
moon breast Parvati

mountain thunder speaks
hair tingling static as the lightning lashes
is neither word of love nor wisdom;
though this be danger: hence thee fear.
Some flowing girl
whose slippery dance
en trances Shiva
—the valley spirit / Anahita,
Sarasvati,
dark and female gate of all the world
water that cuts back quartzflake sand
soft is the dance that melts the
mat-haired mountain sitter
to leap in fire
& make of sand a tree
of tree a board, of board (ideas!)
somebody's rocking chair.
A room of empty sun of peaks and ridges
a universe of junk, all left alone.

The hat I always take on mountains:
When we came back down through Oregon

                    (three years before)
at nightfall in the Siskiyou few cars pass.

A big truck stopped a hundred yards above
        "Siskiyou Stoneware" on the side
the driver said
he recognized my old green hat.
I'd had a ride
                with him two years before
a whole state north
                when hitching down to Portland
                        from Warm Springs.

Allen in the rear on straw
forgot salami and we went on south
all night—in many cars—to Berkeley in the dawn.

        Upper Kern River country now after nine days walk
        it finally rain.
                We ran on that other trail crew
        setting up new camp in the drizzly pine
        cussing & slapping bugs, four days from road,
        we saw McCool, & he said tell that Moorehead
                kiss my ass.

        We squatted smoking by the fire.
                "I'll never get a green hat now"
        the foreman says fifty mosquitoes sitting on the brim

                        they must like green.
        & two more days of thundershower and cold
                (on Whitney hair on end

hail stinging bare legs in the blast of wind
but yodel off the summit echoes clean)

all this comes after:

purity of the mountains and goodwills.
The diamond drill of racing icemelt waters
        and bumming trucks & watching

buildings raze
        the garbage acres burning at the Bay
        the girl who was the skid-row
cripple's daughter—

                out of the memory of smoking pine
the lotion and the spittoon glitter rises
chair turns and in the double mirror waver
the old man cranks me down and cracks a chuckle

                "Your Bubbs Creek haircut, boy."

Boat of a Million Years

The boat of a million years,
    boat of morning,
sails between the sycamores of turquoise,

Dawn white Dutch freighter
in the Red Sea—with a red stack—
heads past our tanker, out toward Ras Tanura,
    sun already fries my shoulder blades, I
      kneel on ragged steel decks chipping paint.
Gray old T-2 tanker and a
    white Dutch freighter,

    boat of the sun,
the abt-fish, the yut-fish,
    play in the waves before it,

salty Red Sea
    dolphins rip sunlight
streak in, swirl and tangle
    under the forward-arching wave roll
of the cleaving bow

    Teilhard said "seize the tiller of the planet" he was
    joking,

We are led by dolphins toward morning.

The Blue Sky

"Eastward from here,

beyond Buddha-worlds ten times as
numerous as the sands of the Ganges
there is a world called
    PURE AS LAPIS LAZULI
its Buddha is called Master of Healing,
    AZURE RADIANCE TATHAGATA"

It would take you twelve thousand summer vacations
driving a car due east all day every day
to reach the *edge* of the lapis lazuli realm of
Medicine Old Man Buddha;
East. Old Man Realm,
East across the sea, yellow sand land
Coyote Old Man land
Silver, and stone blue.

      •

Blue. Belo, "bright colors of the flames"
    flamen / brahman,
    beltane, "blue fire"—
Sky.
    [The dappled cloud zone—
    Sanskrit *sku* "covered"
    skewed (pied)   skewbald (. . . "Stewball")
    skybald / piebald]—

        Horse with lightning feet!
        A mane like distant rain,

the turquoise horse,
a black star for an eye
white shell teeth.

Pony that feeds on the pollen of flowers
may he
make thee whole.
     Heal, hale. . . . whole.

The Spell of the Master of Healing.

Namo bhagavate bhaishajyaguru-vaidurya-
    prabharajaya tathagata arhate samyak
    sambuddhaya tadyatha om bhaishajye
    bhaishajye bhaishajya samudgate
      svāhā.

"I honor the Lord, the Master of Healing,
shining like lapis lazuli, the king, the
Tathagata, the Saint, the perfectly enlightened
one, saying OM TO THE HEALING
TO THE HEALING TO THE HEALER HAIL!
    svāhā."

    •

Shades of blue through the day.
T'u chüeh a border tribe near China
Türc
Turquoise: a hydrous phosphate of aluminum
        a little copper
        a little iron—

    •

In the reign of the Emperor Nimmyo
when Ono-no-Komachi the strange girl poet
was seventeen, she set out looking for her father
who had become a Buddhist wanderer. She took ill
on her journey, and sick in bed one night saw

AZURE RADIANCE THUS-COME MEDICINE
MASTER

in a dream. He told her she would find a hotsprings
on the bank of the Azuma river in the Bandai mountains
that would cure her; and she'd meet her father there.

·

"Enchantment as strange as
the Blue up above" my rose of San Antone

Tibetans say that goddesses have lapis lazuli hair.

Azure   Old French *azur*,
             Persian *lazhward*, "lapis lazuli"
—blue bead charms against the evil eye—

(Tim and Kim and Don and I were talking about
what an awful authoritarian garb Doctors
and Nurses wear, really, how spooky it is.
"What should they wear?"

           —"masks and feathers!")

·

Ramana Maharshi Dream

I was working as a woodcutter by a crossroads—Ko-san was working with me—we were sawing and splitting the firewood. An old man came up the lane alongside a mud wall—he shouted a little scolding at some Zen monks who were piling slash by the edge of the woods. He came over and chatted with us, a grizzled face— neither eastern nor western; or both. He had a glass of buttermilk in his hand. I asked him "Where'd you get that buttermilk?" I'd been looking all over for buttermilk. He said, "At the O K Dairy, right where you leave town."

•

Medicine, measure, "Maya"—

> Celestial. Arched cover . . . *kam.*
> Comrade: sharing the same tent or sky,
> a bent curved bow.

Kama, God of Love, Son of Maya,
> bow of flowers.

•

Shakyamuni would then be the lord of the present world of
> sorrow;

> Bhaishajyaguru
> Yao-Shih Fo
> Yakushi Nyorai,
> "Old Man Medicine Buddha"

The lord of the lost paradise.
        (Glory of morning, pearly gates,
        tlitliltzin, the "heavenly blue.")

                    •

Thinking on Amitabha in the setting sun,

                his *western* paradise—
                impurities flow out away, to west,
                behind us, *rolling,*

                planet ball forward turns into the "east"
                light-years beyond,
                Great Medicine Master;
                land of blue.

        The blue sky

        the blue sky.

        The Blue Sky

        is the land of

        OLD MAN MEDICINE BUDDHA

        where the eagle that flies out of sight

        flies.

II

The Market

San Francisco

Heart of the city
                down town
the country side.

John Muir   up before dawn
packing pears in the best boxes
        beat out the others—to Market
                the Crystal Palace
on the morning milk-run train.

Seattle

Me, milk bottles by bike
Guernsey milk, six percent butterfat
raw and left to rise natural
                ten cents a quart
slipped on the ice turning
                in to a driveway
        and broke all nine bottles.
When we had cows . . .
        a feathery hemlock out back
        by manure pile where
                one cow once
        lay with milk fever
        confusions & worries until the vet come
we do this still dark in the morning—

        •

To town on high thin-wheeled carts.
Squat on the boxtop stall.
Papayas banana sliced fish grated ginger
fruit for fish, meat for flowers
    french bread for ladle
        steamer, tea giant
    rough glaze earthware
        —for brass shrine bowls.

Push through fish
bound pullets lay on their sides
        wet slab
watch us with glimmering eye
        slosh water.
A carrot, a lettuce, a ball of cooked noodle.
    Beggars hang by the flower stall
    give them all some.

Strong women.   Dirt from the hills
        in her nails
valley thatch houses
    palmgroves for hedges
ricefield and thrasher
    to white rice
    dongs and piastre
to market, the
        changes, how much
        is our change:

    •

Seventy-five feet hoed rows equals
one hour explaining power steering
equals two big crayfish =
     all the buttermilk you can drink
= twelve pounds cauliflower
= five cartons greek olives = hitchhiking
     from Ogden Utah to Burns Oregon
= aspirin, iodine and bandages
= a lay in Naples = beef
= lamb ribs = Patna
     long grain rice, eight pounds
equals two kilogram soybeans = a boxwood
         geisha comb
equals the whole family at the movies
equals whipping dirty clothes on rocks
     three days some Indian river
= piecing off beggars two weeks
= bootlace and shoelace
     equals one gross inflatable
     plastic pillows
= a large box of petit-fours, chou-crèmes,
     mangoes, apples, custard apples, raspberries
= picking three flats strawberries
= a christmas tree = a taxi ride
carrots, daikon, eggplant, green peppers
oregano white goat cheese
     = a fresh-eyed bonito, live clams
a swordfish
a salmon
     a handful of silvery smelt in the pocket;

whiskey in cars   out late after dates
old folks eating cake in secret
breastmilk enough,
       if the belly be fed—

& wash down   hose off aisles
reach under fruit stands
     green gross rack
         meat scum on chop blocks
         bloody butcher concrete floor
     old knives sharpened down to scalpels
     brown wrap paper rolls, stiff
         push-broom back
wet spilled food
     when the market is closed
        the cleanup comes
            equals

a billygoat pushing through people
stinking and grabbing a cabbage
arrogant, tough,
he took it—they let him—
Kathmandu—the market

I gave a man seventy paise
in return for a clay pot
of curds
was it worth it?
How can I tell

•

They eat feces
        in the dark
        on stone floors
one-legged monkeys, hopping cows
        limping dogs   blind cats
crunching garbage in the market
        broken fingers
                cabbage
        head on the ground.

Who has young face
        open pit eyes
between the bullock carts and people
        head pivot with the footsteps
                passing by
dark scrotum spilled on the street
        penis laid by his thigh
                torso
turns with the sun.

I came to buy
        a few bananas by the Ganges
while waiting for my wife.

Journeys

Genji caught a gray bird, fluttering. It
was wounded, so I hit it with a coal shovel;
it stiffened, got straight and symmetrical,
and began to grow in size. I took the bird by
the head with both hands and held it as it
swelled, turning the head from side to side.
The bird became a woman, and I was embracing
her. We walked down a dim-lighted stairway
holding hands, then walking more and more swiftly
through an enormous maze, all underground.
Occasionally we touched surface, and redescended.
As we walked I held a map of our route in
mind—but it became increasingly complex—and
just when I was about to lose the picture,
the woman transferred a piece of fresh-tasting apple
from her mouth to mine. Then I woke.

                    •

Through deep forests to the coast,
and stood on a white sandspit looking in:
over lowland swamps and prairies
where no one had ever been
to a view of the Olympic Mountains in a chill clear wind.

                    •

We moved across dark stony ground to the great
wall: hundreds of feet high. What was beyond
it, cows?—then something began to lift up from behind.

I shot my arrows, shot arrows at it, but it came—
until we turned and ran. "It's too big to
fight"—the rising thing a quarter mile across—
it was the flaming pulsing sun. We fled and
stumbled on the bright lit plain.

.

Where were we—
A girl in a red skirt, high heels,
going up the stairs before me in a made-over barn.
Whitewash peeling, we lived together in the loft,
on cool bare boards.
—Lemme tell you something kid—
        back in 1910.

.

Walking a dusty road through plowed-up fields
at forest-fire time—the fir tree hills dry,
smoke of the far fires blurred the air—
& passed on into woods along a pond,
beneath a big red cedar
to a bank of blinding blue wildflowers
and thick green grass on leveled ground
of hillside where our old house used to stand.
I saw the footings damp and tangled,
and thought my father was in jail,
and wondered why my mother never died,
and thought I ought to bring my sister back.

.

High up in a yellow-gold
dry range of mountains—
brushy, rocky, cactussy hills
slowly hiking down—finally can see below,
a sea of clouds.

Lower down, always moving slowly over the
dry ground descending, can see through the breaks
in the clouds: flat land.
Damp green level rice fields, farm houses,
at last to feel the heat and damp.

Descending to this humid, clouded level world:
now I have come to the LOWLANDS.

.

Underground building chambers clogged with refuse
discarded furniture, slag, old nails,
rotting plaster, faint wisps, antique newspapers
rattle in the winds that come forever down the hall;
passing, climbing, and on from door to door.
One tiny light bulb left still burning
        —now the last—
locked *inside* is hell.
Movies going, men milling round the posters
        in shreds
        the movie always running
—we all head in here somewhere;

—years just looking for the bathrooms
huge and filthy, with strange-shaped toilets full of shit.

Dried shit all around, smeared across the walls of the
adjoining room,
and a vast hat rack.

·

With Lew rode in a bus over the mountains—
rutted roads along the coast of Washington
through groves of redwood. Sitting in the
back of an almost-empty bus,
talking and riding through.
Yellow leaves fluttering down. Passing
through tiny towns at times. Damp cabins
set in dark groves of trees.
Beaches with estuaries and sandbars. I brought
a woman here once long ago,
but passed on through too quick.

·

We were following a long river into the mountains.
Finally we rounded a ridge and could see deeper in—
the farther peaks stony and barren, a few alpine trees.
Ko-san and I stood on a point by a cliff, over a
rock-walled canyon. Ko said, "Now we have come to
where we die." I asked him—what's that up there,
then—meaning the further mountains.
"That's the world after death." I thought it looked
just like the land we'd been traveling, and couldn't
see why we should have to die.
Ko grabbed me and pulled me over the cliff—
both of us falling. I hit and I was dead. I saw

my body for a while, then it was gone.

Ko was there too. We were at the bottom of the gorge. We started drifting up the canyon. "This is the way to the back country."

Mā

Hello Boy—

I was very glad to hear from you
I know by the way you write and what you said
That you was just ok.
Yes I know you all have been busy working long hours.
$15.00 isn't bad at all.
I never made but $5.00 a day.
I thought that was good.
Try your damdest to hang on to a little of it
So if you quit you will have a little to go on.
Glad you are satisfied thats all you need.
Guess you need good saws.
I hope you can get them.
They cost a lot too—gee those boots are high.
They should wear real good.
Sounds like you like it up there and like to work in the timber.
I am glad.
One thing don't be drinking too much cut down once in a while.
Ray talked like Walter charged too much a week,
Don't let him cheat you.

Food is getting higher every place.
You buy a couple calves and I'll raise them for you
I am going to raise some more this year.
The little mare looks much better and she leads.
So you cook.
You don't mind that do you.
Just so you had plenty to cook.
Cooking always looked like it was easy for you.
Do your best thats all you can do.

I been planting some more stuff.

After this month I'll quit.
Getting late to plant even now
But I want to see how it works out.
According to the Almanac it isn't too late.
We had a few corn.
Ruby didn't plant anything so she comes over and takes what
she wants.
Vino did get in once, she got in by the dead tree.
Then I had to fix fence.
She hasn't been in since but sure watches my gates.
I am up here at Ray's place right now watering flowers and
trees — they have a few garden stuff.
Few beans, squash, potatoes and couple hills of watermelon.
I told Ruby that Mel and Shafer were up they left last night.
They killed quite a few rabbits.
Mel dried the meat cut it in small pieces — tasted pretty good.
Zip ate some of it and liked it she said, said she was going to
make some.
She has a .22 — keeps it with her all the time.
My old .22 won't even shoot, just snaps.
Guess there is something wrong with it but I sure don't know
anything about it.
But I can shoot.
I killed several rabbits in my garden.

We had a few funerals here lately.
First Pablo died then Gracie Quarto got word her boy was killed
in Viet-Nam.
So the two were buried the same day.
Just lately 9th Sabrina died and was buried here.

There were quite a few from all over.
Frank and his wife sang—that was nice.

Wish I was there to eat some of those wild berries.
I can't see where you will find time to go pick them.
If some one would pick them then you might make some jelly.

All our cattle are falling off.
We had a thunder shower ruined the grass.
A big fire at Antelope Wells, sure was smoky here.
Said lightning started it.
Pretty clear now so they must of put it out.
Been hot here the last couple days.
Rained all around us not a drop fell here.
I am pretty busy since everyone here is gone watering things.

Will Stark told me to tell you he wanted you to go to Oklahoma
      with him.
Said he wanted you to stay with him.
He is going to start moving in September—taking a bull and
      horses first.
He will have to make about 3 trips before his family goes.
They are all going but the big boy.
Will said you was real good when you were with them.
Said I don't mind drinking but I can't stand a drunk.
Mabie the work is hard.
Nothing here same old thing
People allways drinking then dieing.
Don't seem to mind tho.

Well Boy I'll quit writing for now—write when you can.
Be careful. Drink but don't get drunk. (huh).

Tell all hello—all said hello to you—
Charley was telling me she got a letter from you.

By Boy
as ever

Ma.

Instructions

Fuel filler cap
    —haven't I seen this before? The
    sunlight under the eaves, mottled
    shadow, on the knurled rim of
    dull silver metal.

Oil filler cap
    bright yellow,
    horns like a snail
    —the oil's down there—
    amber, clean, it
    falls back to its pit.

Oil drain plug
    so short, from in to out. Best
    let it drain when it is hot.

Engine switch
    off, on. Off, on. Just
    two places. Forever,

    or,   not even one.

Night Song of the Los Angeles Basin

                    Owl
              calls,
              pollen dust blows
         Swirl of light strokes writhing
         knot-tying light paths,

         calligraphy of cars.

Los Angeles basin and hill slopes
Checkered with streetways. Floral loops
Of the freeway express and exchange.

              Dragons of light in the dark
              sweep going both ways
              in the night city belly.
              The passage of light end to end and rebound,
              —ride drivers all heading somewhere—
              etch in their traces to night's eye-mind

              calligraphy of cars.

Vole paths. Mouse trails worn in
On meadow grass;
Winding pocket-gopher tunnels,
Marmot lookout rocks.
Houses with green watered gardens
Slip under the ghost of the dry chaparral,

              Ghost
              shrine to the L. A. River.
              The *jinja* that never was there

is there.
Where the river debouches
the place of the moment
of trembling and gathering and giving
so that lizards clap hands there
—just lizards
come pray, saying
"please give us health and long life."

      A hawk,
      a mouse.

Slash of calligraphy of freeways of cars.

      Into the pools of the channelized river
      the Goddess in tall rain dress
      tosses a handful of meal.

      Gold bellies roil
      mouth bubbles, frenzy of feeding,
      the common ones, the bright-colored rare ones
      show up, they tangle and tumble,
      godlings ride by in Rolls Royce
      wide-eyed in brokers' halls
      lifted in hotels
      being presented to, platters
      of tidbit and wine,
      snatch of fame,

           churn and roil,

      meal gone   the water subsides.

A mouse,
a hawk.

The calligraphy of lights on the night
freeways of Los Angeles

will long be remembered.

Owl
calls;
late-rising moon.

Covers the Ground

"When California was wild, it was one sweet bee-garden . . . "
                                                        John Muir

Down the Great Central Valley's
blossoming almond orchard acres
lines of tree trunks shoot a glance through
          as the rows flash by—

And the ground is covered with
cement culverts standing on end,
house-high & six feet wide
culvert after culvert far as you can see
          covered with
mobile homes, pint-size portable housing, johnny-on-the-spots,
concrete freeway, overpass, underpass,
          exit floreals, entrance curtsies, railroad bridge,
long straight miles of divider oleanders;
scrappy ratty grass and thistle, tumbled barn, another age,

yards of tractors, combines lined up—
new bright-painted units down at one end,
old stuff broke and smashed down at the other,
cypress tree spires, frizzy lonely palm tree,
steep and gleaming
fertilizer tank towers fine-line catwalk in the sky—

          covered with walnut orchard acreage
irrigated, pruned and trimmed;
with palleted stacks of cement bricks
          waiting for yellow fork trucks;

quarter-acre stacks of wornout car tires,
dust clouds blowing off the new plowed fields,
taut-strung vineyards trimmed out even on the top,

cubic blocks of fresh fruit loading boxes,
long aluminum automated chicken-feeder houses,
  spring fur of green weed
  comes on last fall's hard-baked ground,
    beyond "Blue Diamond Almonds"
come the rows of red-roofed houses
& the tower that holds catfood
with a red / white checkered sign

crows whuff over almond blossoms
beehives sit tight between fruit tree ranks
eucalyptus boughs shimmer in the wind—a pale blue hip-roof
house behind a weathered fence—
crows in the almonds
  trucks on the freeways,
    Kenworth, Peterbilt, Mack,
    rumble diesel depths,
like boulders bumping in an outwash glacial river

  drumming to a not-so-ancient text

 "The Great Central Plain of California
 was one smooth bed of honey-bloom
   400 miles, your foot would press
 a hundred flowers at every step
 it seemed one sheet of plant gold;

 all the ground was covered
 with radiant corollas ankle-deep:

bahia, madia, madaria, burielia,
chrysopsis, grindelia,
     wherever a bee might fly —"

us and our stuff just covering the ground.

The Flowing

Headwaters

Head doused under the bronze
        dragon-mouth jet
        from a cliff
        spring—headwaters, Kamo
        River back of Kyoto,
        Cliff-wall statue of Fudo
Blue-faced growling Fudo,

Lord of the Headwaters, making
Rocks of water,
Water out of rocks

.

Riverbed

Down at the riverbed
        singing a little tune.
        tin cans, fork stick stuck up straight,
        half the stones of an old black campfire ring,

The gypsy actors, rags and tatters,
        wives all dancers,
        and the children clowns,
        come skipping down
        hop on boulders,
                clever—free—

Gravel scoop bed of the Kamo
        a digger rig set up on truck bed with
        revolving screen to winnow out the stones
        brushy willow—twists of sand

At Celilo all the Yakima
        Wasco, Wishram, Warmspring,
        catching salmon, talking,
                napping scattered through the rocks

Long sweep dip net held by a
foam-drenched braced and leaning man
on a rickety scaffold rigged to rocks

the whole Columbia River thunders
beneath his one wet plank

the lift and plume
of the water curling out and over,

Salmon arching in the standing spray.

                    •

Falls

Over stone lip
  the creek leaps out as one
  divides in spray and streamers,
  lets it all   go.

Above, back there, the snowfields
  rocked between granite ribs

turn spongy in the summer sun
water slips out under
mucky shallow flows
enmeshed with roots of flower and moss and heather
seeps through swampy meadows
gathers to shimmer sandy shiny flats
then soars off ledges—

Crash and thunder on the boulders at the base
  painless, playing,
  droplets regather
seek the lowest,
      and keep going down
  in gravelly beds.

There is no use, the water cycle tumbles round—

Sierra Nevada
  could lift the heart so high
  fault block uplift
  thrust of westward slipping crust—one way
to raise and swing the clouds around—
  thus pine trees leapfrog up on sunlight
  trapped in cells of leaf—nutrient minerals called together
  like a magic song
  to lead a cedar log along, that hopes
      to get to sea at last and be
          a great canoe.

A soft breath, world-wide, of night and day,
  rising, falling,

The Great Mind passes by its own
  fine-honed thoughts,
  going each way.

Rainbow hanging steady
  only slightly wavering with the
  swing of the whole spill,
      between the rising and the falling,
          stands still.

I stand drenched in crashing spray and mist,
and pray.

·

Rivermouth

Mouth
you thick
vomiting outward sighing prairie
      muddy waters
      gathering all and
      issue it
      end over end
          away from land.
The faintest grade.
Implacable, heavy, gentle,

—O pressing song
      liquid butts and nibbles
      between the fingers—in the thigh—
      against the eye

curl round my testicles
drawn crinkled skin
     and lazy swimming cock.

Once sky-clear and tickling through pineseeds
     humus, moss fern stone
     but NOW

the vast loosing
        of all that was found, sucked, held,
        born, drowned,

sunk sleepily in
to the sea.

       The root of me
       hardens and lifts to you,
       thick flowing river,

       my skin shivers. I quit

       making this poem.

The Black-tailed Hare

A grizzled black-eyed jackrabbit showed me

    irrigation ditches, open paved highway,
                    white line
    to the hill . . .
    bell chill blue jewel sky
              banners,

banner clouds flying:
the mountains all gathered,
    juniper trees on their flanks,
              cone buds,
    snug bark scale
    in thin powder snow
over rock scrabble, pricklers, boulders,

pines and junipers
singing.

The mountains   singing
to gather the sky and the mist
    to bring it down snow-breath
              ice-banners—
    and gather it water
sent from the peaks
    flanks and folds
down arroyos and ditches by highways the water

the people to use it, the
    mountains and juniper
do it for us

            said the rabbit.

With This Flesh

"Why should we cherish all sentient beings?
Because sentient beings
are the roots of the tree-of-awakening.
The Bodhisattvas and the Buddhas are the flowers and fruits.
Compassion is the water for the roots."

Avatamsaka Sūtra

1 A BEACH IN BAJA

" . . . on the twenty-eighth day of September 1539, the very excellent Señor Francisco de Ulloa, lieutenant of the Governor and captain of the armada by grace of the most illustrious Señor Marques de Valle de Oaxaca, took possession of the bay of San Andres and the Bermeja Sea, that is on the coast of this new Spain toward the north, at thirty-three and a half degrees, for the said Marques de Valle in the name of the Emperor our King of Castile, at the present time and in reality,

> placing a hand on the sword,
> saying, that if anyone contradicts this
>   he is ready to defend it;
> cutting trees with his sword,
> uprooting grass,
> removing rocks from one place to another,
> and taking water from the sea;

all as a sign of possession.
. . . —I, Pedro Palenzia, notary public of this armada, write what happened before me."

11 SAN IGNACIO, *Cadacaaman*, "REED CREEK"

Señora Maria Leree is ninety-eight years old,
rests in a dark cool room at full noon.
A century-old grapevine covers the house. Casa Leree.
"She still tries to tell me what to do"
—her daughter Rebecca
lived fifty-five years in Los Angeles,

Dagobert drives beer truck all day every day
and some nights,
from Guerrero Negro to San Ignacio.
Says the salt works at Guerrero Negro
sell most of their salt to Japan;

Rebecca plays a mandolin
"I need some music down here."
Dagobert trucks beer to ranches
all through central Baja
over those rutted roads.
"I have six kids in Guaymas. I
Get over to see them three days a month"

> South of El Arco
> a hummingbird's nest with four eggs;
>> four Mexican black hawks
> a caracara on the top of a cardón
> a bobcat crossing the truck track at twilight
> a wadi full of cheeping evening birds

Cats walk the fan-palm roof.
> Her two sons are painters.
> —"I am a poet."
"You came down here to Baja for

—inspiration? Poeta?"
Yes, on these tracks. Rising early
Dry leather. Deep wells.
    Where we breathe, we bow.

III THE ARROYO

The bulls of Iberia—Europa loves the Father;
India loves the big-eyed Mother Cow,

In the Thyssen Collection in Madrid there is a painting by Simon
Vouet—*The Rape of Europa*—from about 1640. The white bull is
resting on the ground, the woman sweetly on his back. A cheerful
scene, two serving women, three cherubs, stand by to help this
naked lady and the handsome eager bull. His round eyes looking
up and back, flowers twined around his horns. The Goddess thinks
there's nothing she can't handle? Leaving us with modern Europe
and its states and wars.

        The bony cows of Baja.
Body of grass, forbs, brush, browse.
Dried meat. Charqui "jerky";
(Little church up the arroyo,
Leathery twisted ropy Christ
figure racked to dry)
Quechua *ch'arki*:
dried to keep, good years and bad—
        With this flesh—

skinny cow scratching
horny forehead on a mesquite limb—
Sweet breath spiraling outward,

the MUSCLE   jerky.

the SKIN   shoes, saddles, sheaths
the BONES   buttons
the FAT   buckets of lard
HORNS & HOOVES   glue.
Loose vulva, droopy udder;
the MILK   buttermilk babes

    (the hoof of the cow is a trace of the grasslands
    —the print in the grass is the hoof of a cow)

    Mother *Bos*
in her green-grass body at
   Arroyo de Camanjue—arroyo of reeds—

(Five thousand native people lived here,
temedegua, valiant people, Cochimi,
    old rancherias called
Aggvacaamanc—creek of the hawks
Camané caamanc—creek of the cardón cactus
Cahelulevit—running water
Vaba cahel—water of the camp
Cunitca cahel—water of the large rocks
Cahelmet—water and earth.
        cadéu: reed. *aggava*: hawk.)

    A ragged white-bearded vaquero
rides up the dust track, calls
"A su servicio!" with elegance

    Says, "Adiós!"   "Go with God!"

with this meat   I thee feed
with this flesh   I thee wed.

The Hump-backed Flute Player

The hump-backed flute player
        walks all over.
        Sits on the boulders around the Great Basin
        his hump   is a pack.

Hsüan Tsang
        went to India 629 AD
        returned to China 645
        with 657 sūtras, images, mandalas,
        and fifty relics—
        a curved frame pack with a parasol,
        embroidery, carving,
        incense censer swinging as he walked
        the Pamir   the Tarim   Turfan
        the Punjab   the doab
        of Ganga and Yamuna,

Sweetwater, Quileute, Hoh
Amur, Tanana, Mackenzie, Old Man,
Big Horn, Platte, the San Juan

        he carried
            "emptiness"
        he carried
            "mind only"
            vijñaptimātra

The hump-backed flute player
Kokop'ele

        His hump is a pack.

•

In Canyon de Chelly on the north wall up by a cave is the hump-backed flute player lying on his back, playing his flute. Across the flat sandy canyon wash, wading a stream and breaking through the ice, on the south wall, the pecked-out pictures of some mountain sheep with curling horns. They stood in the icy shadow of the south wall two hundred feet away; I sat with my shirt off in the sun facing south, with the hump-backed flute player just above my head. They whispered. I whispered. Back and forth across the canyon, clearly heard.

•

In the plains of Bihar, near Rajgir, are the ruins of Nalanda. The name Bihar comes from "vihara"—Buddhist temple—the Diamond Seat is in Bihar, and Vulture Peak—Tibetan pilgrims come down to these plains. The six-foot-thick walls of Nalanda, the monks all scattered—books burned—banners tattered—statues shattered—by the Türks. Hsüan Tsang describes the high blue tiles, the delicate debates—Logicians of Emptiness—worshippers of Tārā, "Joy of Starlight," naked breasted. She who saves.

•

Ghost bison, ghost bears, ghost bighorns, ghost lynx, ghost pronghorns, ghost panthers, ghost marmots, ghost owls: swirling and gathering, sweeping down,

> Then the white man will be gone.
> butterflies on slopes of grass and aspen—
> thunderheads the deep blue of Krishna

rise on rainbows
and falling shining rain
each drop—
tiny people gliding slanting down:
        a little buddha seated in each pearl—
and join the million waving grass-seed-buddhas
on the ground.

        •

Ah, what am I carrying? What's this load?
        Who's that out there in the dust
        sleeping on the ground?
        With a black hat, and a feather stuck in his sleeve?

        —It's old Jack Wilson,
        Wovoka, the prophet,

        Black Coyote saw the whole world
        In Wovoka's empty hat

        the bottomless sky

        the night of starlight, lying on our sides

        the ocean, slanting higher

        all manner of beings
        may swim in my sea
        echoing up conch spiral corridors

the mirror: countless ages back
dressing   or laughing
what world today?

     pearl crystal jewel
     taming and teaching
     the dragon in the spine

     spiral, wheel,
     or breath of mind

     —desert sheep with curly horns.
     The ringing in your ears

     is the cricket in the stars.

•

Up in the mountains that edge the Great Basin

     it was whispered to me
     by the oldest of trees.

     By the Oldest of Beings
     the Oldest of Trees

     Bristlecone Pine.

     And all night long sung on
        by a young throng

     of Pinyon Pine.

III

The Circumambulation of Mt. Tamalpais

Walking up and around the long ridge of Tamalpais, "Bay Mountain," circling and climbing—chanting—to show respect and to clarify the mind. Philip Whalen, Allen Ginsberg, and I learned this practice in Asia. So we opened a route around Tam. It takes a day.

STAGE ONE

Muir Woods: the bed of Redwood Creek just where the Dipsea Trail crosses it. Even in the dryest season of this year some running water. Mountains make springs.

> Prajñāpāramitā-hridaya-sūtra
> Dhāranī for Removing Disasters
> Four Vows

Splash across the creek and head up the Dipsea Trail, the steep wooded slope and into meadows. Gold dry grass. Cows—a huge pissing, her ears out, looking around with large eyes and mottled nose. As we laugh. "—Excuse us for laughing at you." Hazy day, butterflies tan as grass that sit on silver-weathered fenceposts, a gang of crows. "I can smell fried chicken" Allen says—only the simmering California laurel leaves. The trail winds crossed and intertwining with a dirt jeep road.

TWO

A small twisted ancient interior live oak splitting a rock outcrop an hour up the trail.

> Dhāranī for Removing Disasters
> The Heat Mantra

A tiny chörten before this tree.

Into the woods. Maze fence gate. Young Douglas fir, redwood, a new state of being. Sun on madrone: to the bare meadow knoll. (Last spring a bed of wild iris about here and this time too, a lazuli bunting.)

THREE

A ring of outcropped rocks. A natural little dolmen-circle right where the Dipsea crests on the ridge. Looking down a canyon to the ocean—not so far.

> Dhāranī for Removing Disasters
> Hari Om Namo Shiva

And on to Pan Toll, across the road, and up the Old Mine Trail. A doe and a fawn, silvery gray. More crows.

FOUR

Rock springs. A trickle even now—

> The Sarasvatī Mantra
> Dhāranī for Removing Disasters

—in the shade of a big oak spreading out the map on a picnic table. Then up the Benstein Trail to Rifle Camp, old food-cache boxes hanging from wires. A bit north, in the oak woods and rocks, a neat little saddhu hut built of dry natural bits of wood and parts of old crates; roofed with shakes and black plastic. A book called *Harmony* left there. Lunch by the stream, too tiny a trickle, we drink water from our bota. The food offerings are swiss cheese sandwiches, swede bread with liverwurst, salami, jack cheese, olives, gomoku-no-moto from a can, grapes, panettone with apple-currant jelly and sweet butter, oranges, and soujouki—greek walnuts in grape-juice paste. All in the shade, at Rifle Camp.

FIVE

A notable serpentine outcropping, not far after Rifle Camp.

> Om Shri Maitreya
> Dhāranī for Removing Disasters

SIX

Collier Spring—in a redwood grove—water trickling out a pipe.

> Dhāranī of the Great Compassionate One

California nutmeg, golden chinquapin the fruit with burrs, the chaparral. Following the North Side Trail.

SEVEN

Inspiration Point.

> Dhāranī for Removing Disasters
> Mantra for Tārā

Looking down on Lagunitas. The gleam of water storage in the brushy hills. All that smog—and Mt. St. Helena faintly in the north. The houses of San Anselmo and San Rafael, once large estates . . . "Peacock Gap Country Club"—Rocky brush climb up the North Ridge Trail.

EIGHT

Summit of Mt. Tamalpais. A ring of rock pinnacles around the lookout.

> Prajñāpāramitā-hridaya-sūtra
> Dhāranī for Removing Disasters
> Dhāranī of the Great Compassionate One
>
> Hari Krishna Mantra
> Om Shri Maitreya
> Hari Om Namo Shiva

All about the bay, such smog and sense of heat. May the whole planet not get like this.
Start the descent down the Throckmorton Hogback Trail. (Fern Canyon an alternative.)

NINE

Parking lot of Mountain Home. Cars whiz by, sun glare from the west.

> Dhāranī for Removing Disasters
> Gopala Mantra.

Then, across from the California Alpine Club, the Ocean View Trail goes down. Some yellow broom flowers still out. The long descending trail into shadowy giant redwood trees.

TEN

The bed of Redwood Creek again.

> Prajñāpāramitā-hridaya-sūtra

Dhāranī for Removing Disasters
Hari Om Namo Shiva
Hari Krishna Mantra
Four Vows

—standing in our little circle, blowing the conch, shaking the staff rings, right in the parking lot.

The Canyon Wren

I look up at the cliffs
but we're swept on by downriver
the rafts
wobble and slide over roils of water
boulders shimmer
under the arching stream
rock walls straight up on both sides.
A hawk cuts across that narrow sky hit by sun,

we paddle forward, backstroke, turn,
spinning through eddies and waves
stairsteps of churning whitewater.
Above the roar
hear the song of a Canyon Wren.

A smooth stretch, drifting and resting.
Hear it again, delicate downward song

ti ti ti ti tee tee tee

descending through ancient beds.
A single female mallard flies upstream—

Shooting the Hundred-Pace Rapids
Su Tung P'o saw, for a moment,
it all stand still.
"I stare at the water:
it moves with unspeakable slowness."

Dōgen, writing at midnight,
"mountains flow

water is the palace of the dragon
it does not flow away."

We beach up at China Camp
between piles of stone
stacked there by black-haired miners,
cool in the dark
sleep all night long by the stream.

These songs that are here and gone,
here and gone,
to purify our ears.

Arctic Midnight Twilight
Cool North Breeze With Low Clouds
Green Mountain Slopes, White Mountain Sheep

Dibée

Song

Green mountain walls in blowing cloud
white dots on far slopes, constellations,
slowly changing not stars   not rocks
"by the midnight breezes strewn"
cloud tatters, lavender arctic light
on sedate wild sheep grazing
tundra greens, held in the web of clan
and kin by bleats and smells to the slow
rotation of their Order living
half in the sky—damp wind up from the
whole north slope and a taste of the icepack—

the primus roaring now,
here, have some tea.

A broad bench, slate surfacing
six sheep break out of the gorge
skyline brisk trot scamper

Pellet piles in moss
a spiral horn in the grass
long tundra sweeps and the rise of slopes
to a peak of Doonerak,
white sheep dots on the far green

One chases one, they run in circles
three move away. One cuts a tangent.
On the shade side canyon wall
scree patch rock slides, serried stepped-up
ledges, a host of sheep hang out.
Sunshine across the valley, they choose
the chilly shade. Perched on cliffs
napping, scratching,
insouciant white head droops
over gulfs of air;

Low sun swings through the twenty-four hours
never high, never gone, a soft slant light,
miles of shadows, ever-dappling clouds,

     a sheepskull forehead with its horn prongs
     sitting on a boulder—
     an offer of the flower of a
     million years of nibbling forbs

     to the emptiness of intelligence,

     sheep impermanence, sheep practice,
     sheep shapeshifting—vows of beings—
     Vajra Sheep teaching the Koyukuk waters
     suchness for each—

"The beat of her unseen feet"
which the wild sheep hear
at the roof of the planet, the warp
of the longitudes gathered,
rips in the wind-built tent

of sky-sea-earth cycles, eating the
green of the twenty-four hours,
breaking the cloud-flock flight
with floods of rising, falling,
warmer, cooler, air-mass swirls
like the curls
of Dall sheep horns. The "feet"
of the onward paces of skulls and pellets—
clouds sublimate to pure air
blowing south through passes
feeding the white dot Dall sheep—dew.

     A sheep track followed by a wolf track
     south of the lake.
     A ewe and lamb in the sunshine, the lamb
     tries to nurse, it's too old,
     she lies down.
     In the scoured-out gullies
     thirty-one sheep.

Climbing Midnight Mountain sliding rock
find a sheep trail goes just right:
on the harder scree at the bases of faces,
follow it out, over ledges, find their hidden
sheltered beds.

Sweet rank smell makes the heart beat,
dusty and big pebbles whisked out
so it's softer, shaped,
sheep dreaming place—

     Sheep time.
     All over the world.

At rest in a sheep bed
at the cliff-edge of life and death
over endless mountains
and streams like strips of the sky.

Up the knife ridge
the trail crosses over and heads down a glacier,
tracks fade in the snow.

Sheep gone, and only endless twilight mountains.
Rest awhile among the rocks
arise to descend   to unbuild it again,

and hear the Koyukon riddle:

"It really snowed hard
in opposite directions
on my head

who am I?"

—*dibée*

a mountain sheep.

Under the Hills Near the Morava River

She lay there midst

Mammoth, reindeer, and wolf bones:

Diadem of fox teeth round her brow

Ocher under her hips

26,640 plus or minus 110 years before "now."

Burnt reindeer-pelvis bone bits
in her mouth,

Bones of two men lying by her,
one each side.

Walking the New York Bedrock
Alive in the Sea of Information

Maple, oak, poplar, gingko
New leaves, "new green" on a rock ledge
Of steep little uplift, tucked among trees
Hot sun dapple—
            wake up.

Roll over and slide down the rockface
Walk away in the woods toward
A squirrel, toward
Rare people! Seen from a safe distance.
A murmur of traffic approaching,
Siren howls echoing
Through the gridlock of structures,
Vibrating with helicopters,
      the bass tone
                  of a high jet.

            Leap over the park stone wall
            Dressed fast and light,
            Slip into the migrating flow.

New York like a sea anemone
Wide and waving in the Sea of Economy,
Cadres of educated youth   in chic costume
Step out to the nightlife, good food, after work—
In the chambers of prana-subtle power-pumping
Heartbeat buildings   fired
Deep at the bottom, under the basement,
Fired by old merchant marine
Ex-fire-tenders   gone now from sea

to the ships stood on end on the land:
   ex-seamen stand watch at the stationary boilers,
   give way to computers,
That monitor heat and the power
   webs underground;   in the air;
In the Sea   of Information.

Brisk flesh, keen-eyed, streams of people
Curve round the sweep of street corners
   cardboard chunks tossed up in truckbed.
Delicate jiggle, rouge on the nipple,
       kohl under the eye.

Time and Life buildings — sixty thousand people —
Wind ripples the banners
   stiff shudder shakes limbs on the
   planted trees growing new green,

Glass, aluminum, aggregate gravel,
Iron. Stainless steel.
Hollow honeycomb brain-buildings owned by

Columbia University, the landlord of
Anemone
     colony
Alive, in the Sea of Information

   "Claus the Wild man"
   Lived mostly with Indians,
   Was there as a witness when the old lady
   "Karacapacomont"
   Sold the last bit of Washington Heights, 1701

Down deep grates hear the watercourse,
Rivers that never give up
Trill under the roadbed, over the bedrock.
A bird angles way off a brownstone
Couloir that looks like a route.

Echo the hollowing darkness.
Crisscrossing light threads
Gleam squeals up the side streets,
One growl shadow
   in an egg of bright lights,
Lick of black on the tongue.
Echoes of sirens come down the walled canyons
Foot lifts to the curb and the lights change—

And look up at the gods.
Equitable god, Cclanese god, noble line,
Old Union Carbide god,
Each catching   shares of the squared blocked shadow
Each swinging in sundial arc of the day
            more than the sum of its parts.
The Guggenheims, the Rockefellers, and the Fricks,
Assembling the art of the world, the plate glass
Window lets light in on "the water lilies"
Like fish or planets, people,
Move, pause, move   through the rooms,
White birch leaves shiver in breezes
While guards watch the world,
Helicopters making their long humming trips
Trading pollen and nectar
In the air
     of the
Sea of   Economy,

Drop under the streetworld
Steel squeal of stopping and starting
Wind blows through black tunnels
    spiderwebs, fungus, lichen.

Gingko trees of Gondwanaland. Pictographs,
Petroglyphs, cover the subways—
Empty eye sockets of buildings just built
Soulless, they still wait the ceremony
    that will make them too,
        new, Big
        city Gods,
Provided with conduit, cable and plumbing,
They will light up, breathe cool air,
Breathe the minds of the workers who work there—
The cloud of their knowing
As they soar in the sky, in the air,
Of the Sea
Of Information,

    Cut across alleys and duck beneath trucks.
    "Under Destruction"—trash chair at the curb—
    Stop to gaze on the large roman letters
    Of writing on papers that tell of Economy,

Skilsaw whine slips through the windows
Empty room—no walls—such clear air in the cellar
Dry brick, cooked clay, rusty house bodies
Carbide blade Skilsaw cuts bricks. Squalls
From the steps leading down to the subway.
Blue-chested runner, a female, on car streets,
Red lights block traffic but she like the
Beam of a streetlight in the whine of the Skilsaw,
    She runs right through.

A cross street leads toward a river
North goes to the woods
South takes you fishing
Peregrines nest at the thirty-fifth floor

Street people rolling their carts
     of whole households
Or asleep wrapped in light blue blanket
     spring evening, at dusk, in a doorway,
Eyeballing arêtes and buttresses rising above them,
     con domus, dominion,
          domus,
     condominate, condominium
Towers, up there the
Clean crisp white dress white skin
     women and men
Who occupy sunnier niches,
Higher up on the layered stratigraphy cliffs, get
More photosynthesis, flow by more ostracods,
     get more sushi,
Gather more flesh, have delightful
Cascading laughs,

     —Peregrine sails past the window
     Off the edge of the word-chain
     Harvesting concepts, theologies,
     Snapping up bites of the bits bred by
     Banking
          ideas and wild speculations
     On new information—
          and stoops in a blur on a pigeon,

As the street bottom-feeders with shopping carts
Slowly check out the air for the fall of excess,

Of too much, flecks of extra,
From the higher-up folks in the sky

    As the fine dusk gleam
    Lights a whole glass side of
    Forty some stories

    Soft liquid silver,

Beautiful buildings we float in, we feed in,

    Foam, steel, gray

Alive   in the Sea of Information.

Haida Gwai North Coast, Naikoon Beach, Hiellen River Raven Croaks

Twelve ravens squawk, squork, crork
over the dark tall spruce
  and down to the beach.
Two eagles squabbling, twitter, meeting,
bumping flying overhead

amber river waters
dark from muskeg acids, irons,
murk the stream of tide-wall eagre coming up
over the sandspit, through the drumming surf,
eagles, ravens, seagulls,   over surf,
Salal and cedar at the swelling river,

  wheeling birds make comment:

on gray skies, big swells, storms,
the end of summer, the fall run—
humpy salmon waiting off the bar
  and when they start upstream—

comment
on the flot and jet of sea crud
and the downriver wash of inland
hard-won forest natural trash
from an older wildness, from a climax lowland,
  virgin   system,

Mother
          Earth
loves to love.

Love hard, playing, fighting,
rough and rowdy love-rassling
she can take it, she gives it,

kissing, pounding, laughing—

up from old growth mossy bottoms
twa corbies rork and flutter

the old food
the new food

tangled in fall flood streams.

New Moon Tongue

Faint new moon arc, curl,

again in the west. Blue eve,

deer-moving dusk.

Purple shade in a plant-realm—

a million years of sniffs,

      licks, lip and

reaching tongue.

An Offering for Tārā

I

Have you seen my companion
With her moon-like forehead
         Has she passed this way?

Senge Chhu, the Indus River.
Some land from Gondwana,

crossed the Tethys Sea
and fetched up against Eurasia,
ranges warping out—
Indus, Sutlej, rivers even from before
sat their seats
as mountains rose around them million-yeared.

Now town of Leh.
Tattered prayer flags on the house-roofs—
built on a bajada, a
glacier-flour and outwash gravel fan down from the hills,
built up to be fields for the barley,
all crisscrossed with ditches—

(Some questions rise:
Glaciers, and how high must they be to catch snow and make year-round streams in a land of no rain?
Where was the hearth of high altitude barley and when did it spread?
Did these people move here to escape some tyrant, or because they were crazy and bold?)

Water from the icefields,
"The long wide tongue of the Buddha" led into asides,
divided down to little rock-edged channels—

wanders on the terraces,
passes through barley plots
apples and apricots, poplar stands:
finds its way back to the gorge.

Wild sheep whose horns and skulls
make a woven rooftop shrine,
— hunters came for sheep before farmers or lamas,
but now they move rocks.

Marpa had Milarepa build stone houses many times. People rais-
ing gravel outwash into walls and houses. Walls built within walls,
terrace stepped above terrace—mixing mud, drying brick, moving
rock: to build a *gompa* on some peak or cliff.

Alluvium carried up the slope
shaped into *gompas*, temples,
confidence, patience, good humor
in the work of hands with the stone and grit of the world.

Tabletop mandalas made
by the monks over weeks—
screek screek, goes the rasp as the sand tube
is played like a brush—sand colors,
fine-ground minerals from
cut-banks and outcroppings,
pulverized rocks from the canyons,
monk-artists making vision palaces,

maps of stages of the soul and all its pathways,
out of mountain dust. For the
puja, the ritual, the offering, the meal,

Marpa purifying Milarepa,
"Build it again!" Snapping
snap-lines, setting levels, placing stones.

II

> *In the lofty sky*
> *Is the nest of a vulture*
> *May it remain unchanged.*
> *The unchanged bird,*
> *May you remain unchanged.*

Angdu's parents were still out in the fields so we stepped into a half-built house up the hill, and were served both butter tea and black tea. A little Tārā shrine in a corner, a floor-sitters table and a small blue rug. Catty-corner on a torn-out tarp was something drying, twiggy bunches, caraway seed-heads,

We do the Tārā mantra for the shrine—

Om tāre tuttāre ture swāhā   tāre tāre tāre
　　　Om tāre tuttāre ture swāhā   tāre tāre tāre
Om tāre tuttāre ture swāhā   tāre tāre tāre

•

Tārā's Vow

"Those who wish to attain supreme enlightenment
in a man's body are many . . .

therefore may I,
        until this world is emptied out,
serve the needs of beings
with my body of a woman."

    These steep eroding mountains,
    no place for lakes or meadows
    newest mountains,
    Baby Krishna Himalaya,
    snowy Storehouse Mountains,
    snow-basket Mountains,

    Baby Himalaya loves butter,
    loves dirt,

    baby mountains—Ancient Buddhas—
    naked Blue Samantabhadra,
    Kalachakra, Yamantaka,
    young eroding
    Himalaya,

    alpine fields of blue sheep meadow
        blue sheep love the Himalayas—

    each one thinks the Himalaya
        is hers alone.

    Rock stuff always folding
    turned back in again, re-folded,
    wrapping, twisting in and out like dough.

    "Black as bees are the plaits of your hair"

III

The great Indus river's running
just there by the wall.
      (The far shore
wild salmon spawning
in old mine-tailing gravels down the Yuba)

Led to the kohlrabi, peas and potatoes,
gold-dry barley,
come songbirds,
a village with flat-roofed houses
and a flag in the breeze
always murmuring,

      Space of joy
      in the life of the moment
      Om, Mind, in Phenomena, Hum

The crooked sickle topples alfalfa,
and the sheaves are packed on their backs
husband and wife walk singing
song bounced between voices
down the stone-paved walk
to the storehouse and stables,

      and give some away.

Up in the stone towers and walkways,
apartments and chambers,
wide-ranging cloud chaos
silvery Senge Chhu curving below

fields by the river, white dot houses
        barley laid drying.

Conch blows from the rooftop
monks in maroon
chant, grin and glance,
and a boy who plays leader
makes all the bows,
Tārā, cross-legged, head tilted smiling,
hands shaping "the giving"
red body, gold body, green,

a puja, a potluck
for the whole Himalayan plateau,
—drop of chang on the tongue,
barley dough pinch,
salt tea and sliced apple—
In the temple built above the Indus
demons trample,
intestines tangling, men and women dancing screwing
head of a horse, a bull, all
painted on shadowy walls in the
Buddha hall in the sky.

⋅

(Tārā's love magic

From the boy's heart a red beam of light goes out through his right
ear, enters the nock of his arrow, comes out the arrowhead, and
shines straight to his loved one's vagina—menstrual blood trickles
down, he enters her mind, she becomes full of desire.)

⋅

Cross-legged,
we sit on the wood floor taking
puja, the offering for Tārā,
old monks and a boy bring food
to the music of shawms.
Ibex, antelope, argali sheep, golden eagle,
over mountains and valley,
(summer sleeping on the rooftops,
Indo-Tibetan army unit
camps beside the airport
jeeps clatter up the hill toward Leh)

> *space of joy*
> *in the heart of the moment*
> prayer spins in the crankcase,

Baby Himalaya
loves butter, loves a little taste of dirt,
loves the herdgirls, loves the ibex,

Tārā lady of the stars:

grimy-handed cutting barley,
leading water,
moving stones.

> *On the lofty mountain*
> *Is the nest of a hawk;*
> *On the lofty rock,*
> *The nest of a white hawk;*

> *The unchanged bird,*
> *May you remain unchanged.*

The Bear Mother

She veils herself
        to speak of eating salmon
    Teases me with
        "What do you know of my ways"
    And kisses me through the mountain.

Through and under its layers, its
        gullies, its folds;
    Her mouth full of blueberries,
        We share.

Macaques in the Sky

Walking the trail with Wang Ch'ing-hua, Red Pine, Lo Ch'ing,
and Carole from Nanren Lake, we see a clear spot in the jungle
canopy of leaves—a high point arch of heavy limbs, a lookout on
the forest slope—

A mother monkey sits and nurses,

A couple perching side by side,

A face peeks from another leaf screen, pink cheeks,
shining eyes,

An old male, silver belly, furrowed face,
laid back in a crotch

harsh little cough-calls echo

faces among the leaves,
being ears and eyes of trees
soft hands and haunches pressed on boughs and vines

Then—*wha!*—she leaps out in the air
the baby dangling from her belly,

they float there,

—she fetches up along another limb—
and settles in.

Her
arching like the Milky Way,
mother of the heavens,
        crossing realm to realm
        full of stars

as we hang on beneath with all we have

enjoy her flight.
Drink her light.

Rhesus macaque.

IV

Old Woodrat's Stinky House

The whole universe is an ocean of dazzling light
On it dance the waves of life and death.
                                    a service for the spirits of the dead

•

Coyote and Earthmaker whirling about in the world winds
found a meadowlark nest floating and drifting; stretched it to
cover the waters and made us an earth—

     Us critters hanging out together
     something like three billion years.

     Three hundred something million years
     the solar system swings around
     with all the Milky Way—

     Ice ages come one hundred fifty million years apart
     last about ten million
     then warmer days return—

     A venerable desert woodrat nest of twigs and shreds
     plastered down with ambered urine
     a family house in use eight thousand years,
          & four thousand years of using writing equals
     the life of a bristlecone pine—

     A spoken language works
     for about five centuries,
     lifespan of a douglas fir;
     big floods, big fires, every couple hundred years,
     a human life lasts eighty,
     a generation twenty.

Hot summers every eight or ten,
four seasons every year
twenty-eight days for the moon
day / night   the twenty-four hours

& a song might last four minutes,

a breath is a breath.

.

all this in 5,086 coyote scats:
Pocket gopher, elk, elk-calf, deer, field mouse,
snowshoe hare, ground squirrel, jackrabbit, deer mouse,
pine squirrel, beaver.
Jumping mouse, chipmunk, woodrat, pika.
House cat, flying squirrel. Duck, jay, owl, grebe,
fish, snake, grasshopper, cricket, grass.
Pine nuts, rose seeds, mushrooms, paper, rag, twine, orange peel,
matches, rubber, tinfoil, shoestring, paint rag, two pieces of a
        shirt—
                Greater Yellowstone.

        —And around the Great Basin
        people eating cattail pollen,
        bullrush seeds, raw baby birds,
        cooked ducks and geese,
        antelope, squirrel, beetles, chub, and suckers—
        ten thousand years of living
                —thousands paleo human droppings in the
                        Lovelock Cave—

Great tall woodrat heaps. Shale flakes, beads, sheep scats,
flaked points, thorns,

piled up for centuries
placed under overhangs—caves in cliffs—
at the bottom, antique fecal pellets;
orange-yellow urine-amber.
Shreds of every bush that grew eight thousand years;
                another rain, another name.

Cottontail boy said "Woodrat makes me puke!
Shitting on his grandmother's blankets—
stinking everything up—pissing on everything—
yucky old woodrat!
Makes his whole house stink!"

—Coyote says "You people should stay put here,
     learn your place,
                do good things. Me, I'm traveling on."

Raven's Beak River
At the End

Doab of the Tatshenshini River and the Alsek Lake, a long spit of gravel, one clear day after days on the river in the rain, the glowing sandy slopes of Castilleja blooms & little fox tracks in the moose-print swales, & giant scoops of dirt took out by bears around the lupine roots, at early light a rim of snowy mountains and the ice fields slanting back for miles, I find my way

To the boulders
    on the gravel   in the flowers
At the end of the glacier
    two ravens
Sitting on a boulder
    carried by the glacier
Left on the gravel
    resting in the flowers
At the end of the ice age
    show me the way
To a place to sit
    in a hollow on a boulder
Looking east, looking south
    ear in the river
Running just behind me
    nose in the grasses
Vetch roots scooped out
    by the bears in the gravels
Looking up the ice slopes
    ice plains, rock-fall
Brush-line, dirt-sweeps

on the ancient river
Blue queen floating in
   ice lake, ice throne, end of a glacier
Looking north
   up the dancing river
Where it turns into a glacier
   under stairsteps of ice falls
Green streaks of alder
   climb the mountain knuckles
Interlaced with snowfields
   foamy water falling
Salmon weaving river
   bear flower   blue sky singer
As the raven leaves her boulder
   flying over flowers
Raven-sitting high spot
   eyes on the snowpeaks,
Nose of morning
   raindrops in the sunshine
Skin of sunlight
   skin of chilly gravel
Mind in the mountains, mind of tumbling water,
   mind running rivers,
Mind of sifting
   flowers in the gravels
At the end of the ice age
   we are the bears, we are the ravens,
We are the salmon
   in the gravel
 At the end of an ice age

Growing on the gravels
    at the end of a glacier
Flying off alone
    flying off alone
    flying off alone

Off alone

Earrings Dangling and Miles of Desert

Sagebrush *(Artemisia)*, is of the sunflower family *(Asteraceae)*. (Sage *[Salvia]* is in the family of mint.) The Great Basin sagebrush, our biggest artemisia, *Artemisia tridentata*, grows throughout the arid west. Sagebrush often lives with rabbitbrush *(Chrysothamnus)*, salt-bush *(Atriplex)*, and greasewood *(Sarcobatus)*. As a foursome they typify one of the largest plant communities in North America.

> —brushy, bushy, stringybark cobwebby tangle
> multi-stemmed, forking,
> twiglets jut sidewise, a scatter of silky tiny leaves,
> dry twigs stick up straight;
>   a lizard scooting in the frizzy dust—

It is eaten by sagebrush voles, pygmy rabbits, sage grouse, and pronghorn (which can browse it: the plant contains an oil that inhibits microbes in the rumen of cows so that they cannot digest it. Sheep can eat a little. Elk eat it and belch a lot). It is a home to mourning doves, night hawks, sage thrashers, shrikes, and sage sparrows.

The bark has been used by humans for tens of thousands of years. The shreddy fiber makes bags, nets, shawls, and sandals. It is used by ranchers and Indians alike for firewood. The leaves are burned as a purifying incense or a mosquito-repellant smoke. It is used as a tea for stomach disorders by the Hopi, who call it *wi:'kwapi*. The edible seeds are gathered by the Cahuilla, who also make an herbal tea from it. They call it *wikwat*. Another smaller artemisia, *Artemisia californica*, is used by the Cahuilla for a women's tonic.

Sagebrush: in northern Paiute called *sawabi*, in southern Paiute *sangwabi*.

Artemisia,
who lives across the ranges,
stretching for miles,
   she's always there:
with saltbush and greasewood, with rabbitbrush
and all the little grasses.
Her blue-gray-green—

In Europe, plants of the sagebrush group are known as worm-
wood. The wormwood *absinthium* gives the flick of danger to the
drink absinthe—"sagebrush of the glaciers," said Rimbaud.
Pernod is the same drink minus wormwood. Tarragon's a worm-
wood—

Artemisia is worldwide—thirty species in Japan alone. It's the
mugwort and moxa of China. Wormwood is sacred to Artemis.
Narrow leaves glow silver in her moonlight—

   "She loves to hunt
    in the shadows of mountains
    and in the wind"——

Artem in Greek meant "to dangle" or "earring."
(Well-connected, "articulate," art. . . .)

   Her blue-gray-green
   stretching out there
   sagebrush flats reach to the edge
   bend away—
   emptiness far as the mind can see—

Raincloud maidens come walking
lightning-streak silver,
gray skirts sweeping and trailing—

Hail, Artemisia,
aromatic in the rain,
I will think of you in my other poems.

Cross-Legg'd
for Carole

Cross-legg'd under the low tent roof,
dim light, dinner done,

drinking tea. We live
in dry old west

lift shirts bare skin
lean   touch lips—

old touches.
Love made, poems, makyngs,

always new, same stuff
life after life,

as though Milarepa
four times built a tower of stone

like each time was the first.
Our love is mixed with

rocks and streams,
a heartbeat, a breath, a gaze

makes place in the dizzy eddy.
Living this old clear way

—a sizzle of ash and embers.
Scratchy breeze on the tent fly

one sip tea, hunch on bones,
we two be here   what comes.

Afloat

Floating in a tiny boat
lightly on the water, rock with every ripple,

another skin that slides along the water
hung by sea and sky

green mountains turn to clouds
and slip slow by

two-mile saltwater channel
sucks and coils   with the tide,

kayak like a cricket husk—
        like an empty spider egg case,
like dried kelp fronds,
like a dry cast skin of a snake,
like froth on the lip of a wave,

trembles on the membrane
paddling forward, paddling backward

crossing at an angle to the
roiling shallow bars

the mountain slides, the moon slides,
the waters churn together,
the near bank races onward,

twin kayak paddles turn and glint like wings
casting spume,

there is no place we are
but maybe here

sky and water stitched together
with the oystercatchers screaming steady flight
the kittiwakes deliberate beat of wing
the murres bob up from underworlds
the seals heads dip back to it
the terns erratic dive and splash
the ravens tweet and croak and gurgle in the far-off
outflow alders;

wind ripples westward, the tide goes east,
we paddle east southeast
the world a rush of wings and waters,

up the slopes the mountain glacier
looses icemelt over gravel in a soft far roar
that joins the inlet-basin world of cries and whistles

(and all this realm was under icefields ten miles long,
when my grandfather drove his team
to pick berries at Port Orchard)

the glaciers shift and murmur like the tides
under the constant cross-current
steady drum of bird wings
full of purpose, some direction,
all for what
in the stroke
in the swirl of the float

we are two souls in one body,
two sets of wings, our paddles swing
where land meets water   meets   the sky,

where judges and speechmakers, actresses and carpenters,
drop their masks and go on as they were,
as
petrels, geese, oystercatchers, murrelets,
and small fish fry,

in the tide-suck dark draft sea,
floating in the weaving

of clouds, ice, tides, calls
—only to be here!

The tiny skin boat.

The Dance

"Against its will, energy is doing something productive, like the devil in medieval history. The principle is that nature does something against its own will and, by self-entanglement, produces beauty."

Otto Rössler

Izanami
gave birth to rocks, trees, rivers, mountains, grass
and last, a blazing child
      so burned she died.

      In the land of darkness
      a mass of pollution.

      Ah wash her clear stream

      —skinny little girl with *big* ears
      we have passed through
            passed through,   flesh out of flesh.

    •

"Shining Heavens," Goddess of the Sun,
      her brother flung
            mud and shit and a half-skinned pony through
            the palace,
so she entered a cave—shut it up with a rock—
      made the world dark.

    •

Ame-no-uzume, "Outrageous Heavenly Woman," wrapped
the numinous club-moss of Mr. Kagu round her hips, made

133

a headband from the leaves of nishikigi, bound bamboo grass for her wristlets, and put a sounding-board down before the cave where the Sun Goddess stayed.

She danced and she stamped til it echoed around, she danced like a goddess possessed, pulled out her nipples, pushed her sash down til she showed herself down below, and the Plain of High Heaven shook with the laughs and the cheers and the whistles of thousands of gods who were gathered to watch.

Jean Herbert

•

The whole river. Clear back to each creeklet rock-rimmed,
  all one basin drawing in the threads
pacing down dry riverbeds the dance,
 mai, stomping, stepping on the gravelly bar
step, stop, stamp of the foot. Glide and turn,

   headwaters, mountains,
    breathing icy bliss

diamond-glittered bitty snowcreek
eating the inorganic granite down.

Trees once cooled the air, and clouds, ah, ghost of
   water
   springs gone dry. Hills of Yugoslavia clearcut
    for the Roman fleet
   —don't think all that topsoil's gone
    it only waits.

—slept on river sidebars
    drank from muddy streams
    grains cooked in rock-flour glacier water,
    —dirt left on boulders
    for a sandy heap of years,

and creeks meander   just because they swing.

Stamp of the masked dancer
    pacing tangled channels
        putting salt and gold dust in the sea.

·

Ame-no-uzume-no-mikoto bound up her sleeves with
a cord of heavenly *hi-kage* vine, tied around her head a
head-band of the heavenly *ma-saki* vine, bound to-
gether bundles of sasa leaves to hold in her hands, and
overturning a bucket before the heavenly rock-cave
door, stamped resoundingly upon it. Then she became
divinely possessed, exposed her breasts, and pushed
her skirt-band down to her genitals.

                                        Allan Grapard

·

Laughter roared like thunder
    through the plains of heaven
and the hidden
    Goddess of the Sun,
    Amaterasu,
    peeked out round the rock.

All the little faces of the gods gleamed
                white   in the light!
                                            omoshiri.

                •

                        Herbert   *Grapard*

Around her head: nishikigi leaves   masaki vines

In her hands: sasa

As wristlets: sasa

sleeves tied w/:   hi-kage vine

around her hips: club moss

                •

    Ame no uzume.
    What did she wear?
            What leaves in her hair?

    How far did she push her skirt down?

We Wash Our Bowls in This Water

"The 1.5 billion cubic kilometers of water on the earth are split by photosynthe-sis and reconstituted by respiration once every two million years or so."

A day on the ragged North Pacific coast get soaked by whipping mist, rainsqualls tumbling, mountain mirror ponds, snowfield slush, rock-wash creeks, earfulls of falls, sworls of ridge-edge snowflakes, swift gravelly rivers, tidewater crumbly glaciers, high hanging glaciers, shore-side mud pools, icebergs, streams looping through the tideflats, spume of brine, distant soft rain drooping from a cloud,

sea lions lazing under the surface of the sea—

> *We wash our bowls in this water*
> *It has the flavor of ambrosial dew—*

•

Beaching the raft, stagger out and shake off wetness like a
     bear,
stand on the sandbar, rest from the river   being

upwellings, sideswirls, backswirls
curl-overs, outripples, eddies, chops and swells
wash-overs, shallows   confluence turbulence   wash-seam
wavelets, riffles, saying

"A hydraulic's a cross between a wave and a hole,
     —you get a weir effect.
Pillow-rock's a total fold-back over a hole,
     it shows spit on the top of the wave

a haystack's a series of waves at the bottom of a tight
    channel
    there's a tongue of the rapids—the slick tongue—the
    'v'—
some holes are 'keepers,' they won't let you through;
eddies, backflows, we say 'eddies are your friends.'
Current differential, it can suck you down
vertical boils are straight-up eddies spinning,
herringbone waves curl under and come back.
Well, let's get going, get back to the rafts."
        Swing the big oars,
                head into a storm.

> *We offer it to all demons and spirits*
> *May all be filled and satisfied.*
> *Om makula sai svaha!*

    •

Su Tung-p'o sat out one whole night by a creek   on the slopes of
Mt. Lu. Next morning he showed this poem to his teacher:

    The stream with its sounds   is a long broad tongue
    The looming mountain   is a wide-awake body
    Throughout the night   song after song
    How can I   speak at dawn.

Old Master Chang-tsung approved him. Two centuries later
Dōgen said,
    "Sounds of streams and shapes of mountains.
    The sounds never stop and the shapes never cease.
    Was it Su who woke
    or was it the mountains and streams?

Billions of beings see the morning star
and all become Buddhas!
If *you*, who are valley streams and looming
mountains,
can't throw some light on the nature of ridges and rivers,

who can?"

The Mountain Spirit

Ceaseless wheel of lives
ceaseless wheel of lives

red sandstone;
gleaming dolomite

ceaseless wheel of lives

red sandstone and white dolomite.

Driving all night south from Reno
through cool-porched Bridgeport,
past Mono Lake's pale glow,
past tongues of obsidian flow stopped chill,
and the angled granite face
of the east Sierra front—

        Ah. Here I am arrived in Bishop,
Owens Valley, called Payahu Nadu not so long ago.

Ranger Station on main street,
"I'm a traveler.
I want to know the way
to the White Mountains,
& the bristlecone pines."
She gives me maps. "Here. The trail
to the grove at timberline
where the oldest living beings
thrive on rock and air."

"—Thank you for your help."

I go to the pass, turn north,
end of day, climbing high,
find an opening where a
steep dirt side road halts.
A perch in the round dry hills,
prickly pinyon pine boughs shade,
a view to the Last Chance range,
& make a camp.

Nearby, a rocky point.
          Climb it,
passing a tidy scat-arrangement on a ledge,
stand on a dark red sandstone strata outcrop at the edge.
Plane after plane of desert ridges
darkening eastward into blue-black haze.

A voice says

"You had a bit of fame once in the city
for poems of mountains,
          here it's real."

What?

"Yes. Like the lines

> *Walking on walking*
> *under foot   earth turns*

But what do you know of minerals and stone.
For a creature to speak of all that scale of time—what for?

Still, I'd like to hear that poem."

               I answer back,
"— Tonight is the night of the shooting stars,
Mirfak the brilliant star of Perseus
        crosses the ridge at midnight

I'll read it then."

        Who am I talking to?   I think,
walk back to camp.

                •

Evening breeze up from the flats
from the valleys "Salt" and "Death"—
Venus and the new moon sink in a deep blue glow
        behind the Palisades to the west,
needle-clusters shirring in the wind—
listen close, the sound gets better.

Mountain ranges violet haze back fading in the east
puffs of sailing dark-lit cloud, a big owl's
swift soft whip between the trees,
unroll the bedding, stretch out blankets on the
crunchy dry pine needles sun-warm
        resinous ground.

Formations dip and strike my sleep.

. . . .

—Approaching in a dream:

        "Bitter ghosts that kick their own skulls like a ball
        happy ghosts that stick a flower

into their old skull's empty eye—
'good and evil'
—that's another stupid dream—
for streams and mountains
clouds and glaciers,
is there ever an escape?

Erosion always wearing down;
shearing, thrusting, deep plates crumpling,

still uplifting—ice-carved cirques
dendritic endless fractal streambed riffs on hillsides

—bitter ghosts that kick their own skulls like a ball
what's it all for?"

A meteor swift and streaking
like a tossed white pebble
arcing down the sky—

the Mountain Spirit stands there.
Old woman? white ragged hair?
in the glint of Algol, Altair, Deneb,
Sadr, Aldebaran—saying, "I came to hear—"

I can't say no: I speak

The Mountain Spirit

Walking on walking,
under foot   earth turns

Streams and mountains never stay the same.

Walking on walking,
    under foot   earth turns

Streams and mountains never stay the same.

Into earth   rock dives.

As the mountains lift and open
underground out,
     dust over seashell, layers of ooze,
display how it plays.

Buttresses fractured, looming,
friction only, soon to fall, each face
a heap of risks
talus slopes below
flakes weathered off the buried block,
      tricked off an old pluton,
and settle somewhere, ever lower down —
gives a glimpse
of streaks and strains, warp and slide,
abraded gritty mudwash glide
    where cliffs lean
       to the raven-necklace sky —

    Calcium spiraling shells,
no land plants then when
sands and stones flush down the
barren flanks of magma-swollen uplands
slurry to the beach,
ranges into rubble, old shores buried by debris
a lapping trough of tide flats and lagoons
lime-rich wave-wash soothing shales and silts
a thousand miles of chest-deep reef
seabottom riffled, wave-swirled, turned and tilled

by squiggly slime-swimmers many-armed,
        millions of tiny different tracks
        crisscrossing through the mud —

trilobite winding salt sludge,
calcite ridges, diatom babies drifting home,
swash of quartzy sand
        three hundred million years
                be rolling on   and then

ten million years ago an ocean floor
glides like a snake beneath the continent crunching up
old seabed till it's high as alps.
Sandstone layers script of winding tracks
        and limestone shines like snow
        where ancient beings grow.

"When the axe-strokes stop
        the silence grows deeper —"

Peaks like Buddhas   at the heights
        send waters streaming down
to the deep center of the turning world.

And the Mountain Spirit always wandering
        hillsides fade like walls of cloud
        pebbles smoothed off sloshing in the sea

        old woman mountain hears
shifting sand
        tell the wind
                "nothingness is shapeliness"

Mountains will be Buddhas then

when — bristlecone needles are green!
Scarlet penstemon
              flowers are red!

(Mountains feed the people too
stories from the past
              of pine-nut gathering baskets quickly full
              of help at grinding, carrying, healing —)

Ghosts of lost landscapes
              herds and flocks,
                            towns and clans,
great teachers from all lands
tucked in Wovoka's empty hat,
              stored in Baby Krishna's mouth,
                            kneeling for tea
in Vimalakīrti's one small room.

Goose flocks
     crane flocks
              Lake Lahontan come again!

     Walking on walking,
     under foot   earth turns.

•

The Mountain Spirit whispers back:
"All art and song
is sacred to the real.
As such."

Bristlecone pines live long

on the taste of carbonate,
                    dolomite,

spiraled standing coiling
dead wood with the living,
four thousand years of mineral glimmer
spaced out growing in the icy airy sky
white bones under summer stars.

—The Mountain Spirit and me

like ripples of the Cambrian Sea

dance the pine tree

old arms, old limbs, twisting, twining

scatter cones across the ground

stamp the root-foot DOWN

                    and then she's gone.

Ceaseless wheel of lives
red sandstone and white dolomite.

        A few more shooting stars
        back to the bedroll, sleep till dawn.

Earth Verse

Wide enough to keep you looking

Open enough to keep you moving

Dry enough to keep you honest

Prickly enough to make you tough

Green enough to go on living

Old enough to give you dreams

Finding the Space in the Heart

I first saw it in the sixties,
driving a Volkswagen camper
with a fierce gay poet and a
lovely but dangerous girl with a husky voice,

we came down from Canada
on the dry east side of the ranges. Grand Coulee, Blue
Mountains, lava flow caves,
the Alvord desert—pronghorn ranges—
and the glittering obsidian-paved
dirt track toward Vya,
seldom-seen roads late September and
thick frost at dawn; then
follow a canyon and suddenly open to
        silvery flats that curved over the edge

        O, ah! The
        awareness of emptiness
        brings forth a heart of compassion!

We followed the rim of the playa
to a bar where the roads end
and over a pass into Pyramid Lake
from the Smoke Creek side,
by the ranches of wizards
who follow the tipi path.
The next day we reached San Francisco
in a time when it seemed
the world might head a new way.

And again, in the seventies, back from
Montana, I recklessly pulled off the highway
took a dirt track onto the flats,
got stuck—scared the kids—slept the night,
and the next day sucked free and went on.

Fifteen years passed. In the eighties
With my lover I went where the roads end.
Walked the hills for a day,
looked out where it all drops away,
discovered a path
of carved stone inscriptions tucked into the sagebrush

      "Stomp out greed"
      "The best things in life are not things"

words placed by an old desert sage.

Faint shorelines seen high on these slopes,
long gone Lake Lahontan,
cutthroat trout spirit in silt—
Columbian Mammoth bones
four hundred feet up on the wave-etched
      beach ledge; curly-horned
          desert sheep outlines pecked into the rock,

and turned the truck onto the playa
heading for know-not,
bone-gray dust boiling and billowing,
mile after mile, trackless and featureless,
let the car coast to a halt
on the crazed cracked

flat hard face where
winter snow spirals, and
summer sun bakes like a kiln.
Off nowhere, to be or not be,

> all equal, far reaches, no bounds.
> Sound swallowed away,
> no waters, no mountains, no
> bush no grass and
> > because no grass
> no shade but your shadow.
> No flatness because no not-flatness.
> No loss, no gain. So—
> nothing in the way!
> — the ground is the sky
> the sky is the ground,
> no place between, just

> wind-whip breeze,
> tent-mouth leeward,
> time being here.
> We meet heart to heart,
> leg hard-twined to leg,
> > with a kiss that goes to the bone.
> Dawn sun comes straight in the eye. The tooth
> of a far peak called King Lear.

Now in the nineties desert night
    —my lover's my wife—
old friends, old trucks, drawn around;
great arcs of kids on bikes out there in darkness
    no lights—just planet Venus glinting
by the calyx crescent moon,

and tasting grasshoppers roasted in a pan.

> They all somehow swarm down here—
> sons and daughters in the circle
> eating grasshoppers grimacing,

singing sūtras for the insects in the wilderness,

—the wideness, the
foolish loving spaces

full of heart.

> *Walking on walking,*
> *under foot   earth turns*

> *Streams and mountains never stay the same.*

> The space goes on.
> But the wet black brush
> tip drawn to a point,
>   lifts away.

Marin-an 1956–Kitkitdizze 1996

The Making of *Mountains and Rivers Without End*

As a student at Reed College I had the good fortune to study with the brilliant polymath Lloyd Reynolds, who was—among many things—a remarkable calligrapher in the Renaissance Italic mode. It was from Lloyd I learned to appreciate the pen, whether reed, turkey feather, or carefully hand-ground alloy steel tip. One of Lloyd's students was Charles Leong, a Chinese-American veteran back from World War II and studying on the GI Bill. He was already an accomplished seal carver and brush calligrapher of Chinese; with Charlie as my guide, I learned to hold the brush as well as the pen.

I had been introduced to the high snow peaks of the Pacific Northwest when I was thirteen and had climbed a number of summits even before I was twenty: I was forever changed by that place of rock and sky. East Asian landscape paintings, seen at the Seattle Art Museum from the age of ten on, also presented such a space. While at Reed I stumbled onto Ernest Fenollosa's *Epochs of Chinese and Japanese Art*, which gave me further guidance into Asian art. Fenollosa also led me to the translations of Ezra Pound.

After a brief spell of graduate study in anthropological linguistics, I entered graduate school in Oriental languages at the University of California at Berkeley. I also signed up for a class in sumi—East Asian brush painting—in the art department. The instructor was an intense, diminutive Japanese man named Chiura Obata. Obata had us grinding ink seriously and working with an array of brushes; we learned by trying to match his fierce, swift strokes that made pine needles, bamboo stalks, eucalyptus leaves appear as if by magic on the white paper. He was a naturalized citizen who had been in an internment camp—I learned little else about him. Though I lacked talent, my practice with soot-black ink and brush tuned my eye for looking more closely at paintings. In museums and through books I became aware of how the energies of mist, white water, rock formations, air swirls—a chaotic universe where everything is in place—are so much a part of the East Asian painter's world. In one book I came upon a reference to a hand scroll *(shou-chuan)* called *Mountains and Rivers Without End*. The name stuck in my mind.

While at Berkeley I spent summers working in the mountains, in

National Parks or Forests. Two seasons on lookouts (Crater Mountain in 1952, Sourdough Mountain in 1953) in what was then the Mount Baker National Forest, not far south of the Canadian border, gave me full opportunity to watch the change of mood over vast landscapes, light moving with the day—the countless clouds, the towering cumulus, black thunderstorms rolling in with jagged lightning strikes. The prolonged stay in mountain huts also gave me my first opportunity to seriously sit cross-legged, in the practical and traditional posture of Buddhist meditation. Back in Berkeley, I became acquainted with the warm, relaxed, familial, and devotional Buddhism of traditional Asia in the atmosphere of the Berkeley Buddhist church, presided over by Reverend Kanmo Imamura and his gracious and tireless wife, Jane. Their Jodo-shin, or "Pure Land," Buddhism is one of infinite generosity that had come to California with the Japanese immigrants of the early twentieth century. In Berkeley it was open to all. Jodo-shin and Zen are both in the Mahayana tradition; I soaked up Mahayana sūtras and traditional commentaries, Chinese and Japanese Ch'an texts, and Vajrayana writing through those years, taking delight in their scale of imagination and their fearless mytho-psychological explorations.

Thoughts of that time, along with a half year spent working as a logger in eastern Oregon, took shape in a poem sequence called *Myths and Texts*. This sequence was my first venture into the long poem and the challenge of interweaving physical life and inward realms. I studied Oriental languages and practiced Chinese calligraphy with the brush while finishing *Myths and Texts*. The final touches were done in a small abandoned cabin I found in Marin County, California, in early 1956.

My interest in Zen led me to the lectures of Alan Watts, founder of the Academy of Asian Studies in San Francisco, and we came to be friends on the basis of our shared taste for Italic calligraphy as much as our Buddhist interests. In the winter of 1955–56 a remarkable artist from Japan, Saburo Hasegawa, was in residence at the Academy of Asian Studies. I attended some of Hasegawa's lectures. I never saw him wearing Western clothes: he was always in formal kimono and *hakama*. He spoke of East Asian landscape painting as a meditative exercise. I think he once said that the landscape paintings were for Zen as instructively and deeply Buddhist as the tankas and mandalas are for Tibetan Buddhism.

At some point Hasegawa heard that I had never tasted the ceremonial powdered green tea, and he delightedly invited me to his apartment. I still remember the day, April 8, 1956, because it was also the Buddha's birthday. He frothed up the tea with a bamboo whisk, we chatted, and he talked at length about the great Japanese Zen monk painter Sesshū. As I left that day I resolved to start another long poem that would be called *Mountains and Rivers Without End.*

One month later I headed west for the East on a Japanese passenger-freighter. In Kyoto I lived in the Rinzai Zen temple compound of Sho-koku-ji. I immediately entered the local hilly forests, found the trails and shrines, and paid my respects to the local *kami.* In my small spare time I read geology and geomorphology. I came to see the yogic implications of "mountains" and "rivers" as the play between the tough spirit of willed self-discipline and the generous and loving spirit of concern for all beings: a dyad presented in Buddhist iconography as the wisdom-sword-wielding Manjushri, embodying transcendent insight, and his partner, Tārā, the embodiment of compassion, holding a lotus or a vase. I could imagine this dyad as paralleled in the dynamics of mountain uplift, subduction, erosion, and the planetary water cycle.

I began to attend Nō performances, and became an aficionado of Nō history and aesthetics. Over ten years I was able to attend a large number of plays, seeing some of them several times over. Nō is a gritty but totally refined high-culture art that is in the lineage of shamanistic performance, a drama that by means of voice and dance calls forth the spirit realms. I began to envision *Mountains and Rivers* through the dramatic strategies of Nō. The great play *Yamamba* ("Old Mountain Woman") especially fasci-nated me. But I never lost my sense of belonging to North America, and I kept nourishing the images and practices that kept me connected to a sense of the ancient, sacred Turtle Island landscape.

Most of the sixties I spent in Japan. One break was to work nine months on a tanker that went between Persian Gulf and mid-Pacific oil ports. The ocean rocked me. When I got back to Kyoto, Cid Corman was there and had started publishing *Origin.* Early sections of *Mountains and Rivers* appeared there. Others came out in James Koller's *Coyote's Journal.* A visit to the United States in 1964 got me back into the High Sierra, a refreshing return to the realm of rock and ice. In the course of that visit I showed Donald Allen, the editor, translator, and publisher, what I had been up to. He brought out a small book of the sections to date, under the title *Six Sections from Mountains and Rivers Without End.*

Although my main reason for being in Kyoto was to do Zen Buddhist practice, I was also fortunate enough to make contact with Yamabushi, the Mountain Buddhists, and I was given a chance to see how walking the landscape can become both ritual and meditation. I did the five-day pilgrimage on the Omine ridge and established a tentative relationship with the archaic Buddhist mountain deity Fudo. This ancient exercise has one visualizing the hike from peak to valley floor as an inner linking of the womb and diamond mandala realms of Vajrayana Buddhism.

I was now studying under the Rōshi of Daitoku-ji and had moved into my own place, a ten-minute walk from the monastery. I shared the little house with a highly cultured, mature woman named Yaeko Hosaka Nakamura, a student of Nō singing. For more than five years I was soaked in the *utai* chants from *Yamamba* and other Nō plays. Her full, strong voice belted out the eerie melodies from her room upstairs. I even tried chanting with her, but soon gave up.

I got to see rare Japanese and Chinese scrolls in the richly endowed Buddhist temples of Kyoto, especially those of Daitoku-ji. Poems for *Mountains and Rivers* kept showing up at the rate of about one a year. I was writing other poems at the same time, but in a different and more lyrical mode.

In 1969 I returned to live on Turtle Island. More sections got written and they often appeared in Clayton Eshleman's *Caterpillar.* (Eshleman had been a number of years in Kyoto and it was there I first met him.) Later sections have appeared in his magazine *Sulfur.* I moved with my family to the Sierra Nevada and developed a farmstead in the pine-oak forest.

While giving readings and talks around the country through the seventies and eighties, I was able to visit most of the major collections of Chinese paintings in the United States. In Cleveland I saw the Sung Dynasty *Streams and Mountains Without End*, the one that is described here in the opening section. The curators at the Freer generously let me have two private viewings of Lu Yüan's Ch'ing scroll called *Mountains and Rivers Without End*—most likely the very one that first came to my attention. I roamed the Nelson Gallery in Kansas City, the Honolulu Academy of Arts, the Boston Museum of Fine Arts; and in Europe the British Museum and the Stockholm National Museum. I had always made good use of The Asian Art Museum of San Francisco. Finally I managed to get to the Palace Museum in Beijing and the huge Palace Museum in Taipei, where I was deeply moved to see calligraphy from the hand of Su Shih himself. Gazing at these many paintings was each time a mysteriously enlarging experience.

In the late seventies my thinking was invigorated by the translations from Dōgen's *Treasury of the True Law* just then beginning to come out. His *Mountains and Waters Sūtra* is a pearl of a text. It made me think more about rivers. What with mountaineering and seasonal labor I had plenty of firsthand experience with mountains, so now I studied waters, spinning and dashing down many a rapids in rowdy and convivial company. And, starting from when I returned to the Pacific coast, I gradually extended my range of walked-in landscapes. North to Alaska, as far as the Brooks Range and the Arctic Sea; south to the Southwestern U.S. and the length of Baja California. Overseas I spent time in the Central Australian Desert; traveled in the Himalayan nation of Ladakh; visited China; and made a brief visit to the wilder parts of Taiwan. I crossed the pass and went east into the Great Basin frequently. I went back into old High Sierra haunts and took some sweet and reflective treks.

At some point I became aware of the powerful light-filled watercolor paintings and color woodblocks of California mountain landscapes that had been done by my old teacher Chiura Obata. It turned out that he had explored and sketched the Sierra high country many times, beginning in the 1920s.

During the last twenty years my sense of the poem has also been enlarged by several other experiences: working/walking visits to major urban centers; working alongside my brilliant and cranky neighbors in the Sierra foothills; laboring hands-on at forest and ecosystem management chores; studies of landscape and forest ecology; the lessons of our local watershed, getting down to the details of its tiniest rivulets and hillocks; and the joys and teachings that come with family life—my wife Carole and my sons and daughters.

By the 1990s I was teaching part-time at the University of California at

Davis, 108 miles away in the broad Sacramento Valley. I turned my full attention to the thought of *Mountains and Rivers*. In April 1996, on the fortieth anniversary of my tea with Saburo Hasegawa, a few of us old mountain-Buddhist-poetry-green-avant-garde types got together again in San Francisco: to remember old comrades, to declare this project ended, and to drink a cup to "the supreme theme of art and song." The T'ang poet Po Chü-i said, "I have long had the desire that my actions in this world and any problems caused by my crazy words and extravagant language [*kyōgen kigo*] will in times to come be transformed into a clarification of the Dharma, and be but another way to spread the Buddha's teachings." May it be so!

People used to say to me, with a knowing smile, "*Mountains and Rivers* is endless, isn't it?" I never thought so. Landscapes are endless in their own degree, but I knew my time with this poem would eventually end. The form and the emptiness of the Great Basin showed me where to close it; and the boldness of my young people, who ate unlikely manna in the wilderness, how. This poem, which I have come to think of as a sort of sūtra—an extended poetic, philosophic, and mythic narrative of the female Buddha Tārā—is for them.

Notes

Endless Streams and Mountains

Colophons, reproduction of the handscroll, and commentary can be found in Sherman Lee and Wen Fong, *Streams and Mountains Without End* (1967). Most of the colophon / poem translations are my own.

The East Asian landscape paintings invite commentary. In a way the painting is not fully realized until several centuries of poems have been added.

A note on Chinese landscape paintings: There were very early scenes of hills and woods in China, on silk or plastered walls, but they were full of deer and other animals, or dream creatures, or people, or some combination. Paintings of large vistas did not appear until around the tenth century. This was after two and a half millennia of self-aware civilization in the basins of the Ho and Chiang. They are at their most vigorous from mid-Sung through the Yüan and early Ming—exactly when much of China was becoming deforested.

After the Yüan dynasty large-scale "Mountains and Waters" paintings became less important, and the painter's eye moved closer; some call them "Rocks and Trees" paintings. Later paintings drew even closer to give us pictures of "Birds and Flowers," *hua-niao*, precise and lovely, and superb sumi sketches of insects, gourds, melons, and leaves.

Old Bones

This poem is for Paul Shepard.

Three Worlds, Three Realms, Six Roads

The title derives from Buddhist terms. The "three worlds" are periods of time: past, present, and future. The "three realms," *triloka*, describe the universe in terms of desire, form, and formlessness. The "six paths" are territories of psychological passage: the hells, the animals, the humans, delightful gods and goddesses, angry warrior-geniuses, and hungry ghosts.

Bubbs Creek Haircut

This poem is for Locke McCorkle.

Shiva, the "Destroyer" of the Hindu trinity, is practicing in the mountains. His lover and yogic partner is Parvati.

The Blue Sky

This section is an exploration of some of the lore of healing as found in Mahayana Buddhism and in Native North America. Bhaishajyaguru (Sanskrit)—the "Medicine Buddha"—is known in Japan as Yakushi Nyorai. He holds a tiny medicine bottle in the palm of one hand. Eons ago he made a vow to work for the welfare and healing of all sentient beings.

Another element is the ancient lore of the protective and healing powers of the color blue and of certain blue stones.

The character *k'ung*, used for the Buddhist term *shunyata* or "emptiness" in Chinese, also means "sky." I was once told by a Native California elder that the diagnostic and healing hand of a "trembling-hand healer's hand" was guided by an eagle so high up in the sky as to be out of sight.

The Hump-backed Flute Player

Ancient rock art—petroglyphs—of a walking flute-playing figure, sometimes with a hump on his back, are found widely in the Southwest and into Mexico. These images are several thousand years old. There is a Hopi secret society that takes the Flute-player as its emblem. Some of the figures have an erect penis, and some have feelers on their heads that look like insect antennae.

It has been suggested that the hump is possibly a pack, and that the figure may represent Aztec or Toltec wandering traders, who once came up into the Southwest with trade items. In Peru even today you can see young men with a sort of sling-pack on their backs, carrying a load and playing the flute while walking.

Gary Paul Nabhan and I were reflecting on Kokop'ele a few years ago, and were entertained by the thought that it might be *seeds* that he was carrying! As a possible emblem of genetic diversity his work is not over: guardianship and preservation, not just of plants and animals, but of peoples and cultures as well.

Hsüan Tsang, the Buddhist scholar-pilgrim, brought back the famed "Heart Sutra"—the one-page condensation of the whole philosophy of transcendent wisdom—in his pack. Once he had translated it into Chinese it was set in movable type—the first text to be printed this way, it is said.

Note: "White man" here is not a racial designation, but a name for a certain set of mind. When we all become born-again natives of Turtle Island, then the "white man" will be gone.

The Circumambulation of Mt. Tamalpais
This poem is for Philip Whalen and Allen Ginsberg.

Walking meditation, circumambulation, *pradakshina*, is one of the most ancient human spiritual exercises. On such walks one stops at notable spots to sing a song, or to chant invocations and praises, such as mantras, songs, or little sūtras.

The Canyon Wren
This poem is for James and Carol Katz.

The Stanislaus River comes out of the central Sierra. The twists and turns of the river, the layering, swirling stone cliffs of the gorges, are cut in nine-million-year-old latites. We ran the river to see its face once more before it went under the rising water of the New Mellones Dam. The song of the canyon wren stayed with us the whole time.

Arctic Midnight Twilight . . .
This poem is for Peter Coyote.

Under the Hills Near the Morava River
Excavations by Bohuslav Klima at the Dolni Vestonice site in the Pavlovske Kopce hills of southern Moravia (Czech Republic).

Haida Gwai North Coast, Naikoon Beach
This poem is for Sherman Paul.

An Offering for Tārā
Out of the upper Indus River watershed, on the Western Tibetan Plateau, around Ladakh and its main town of Leh.

Tārā, "She Who Brings Across," is a female Buddha of both Compassion and Wisdom. She is one of the most revered figures in Buddhism, especially in Tibet, Mongolia, and Nepal.

Raven's Beak River
This poem is for Edward Schafer.

Earrings Dangling and Miles of Desert
This poem is for Ursula Le Guin.

The Dance
Otto Rössler as cited in James Gleick, *Chaos: Making a New Science* (1987), 142.

Jean Herbert's *Kojiki* translation from his *Shinto* (1967).

Allan Grapard's translation from the same episode in "Visions of Excess" *Japanese Journal of Religious Studies* 18:1 (March 1991).

We Wash Our Bowls in This Water
This poem incorporates a Zen training-hall meal verse. Su Shih (Su Tung-p'o) was the great eleventh-century Chinese poet and Zen adept. This was his "enlightenment poem." The translation is my own. Dōgen gave a lecture on it to his students some two centuries later.

"Two million years": Preston Cloud and Aharon Gibor, "Oxygen Cycle," *Biosphere* (San Francisco: Scientific American Books/Freeman, 1970).

The Mountain Spirit
This poem somewhat follows the Nō play *Yamamba* (Old Mountain Woman), a play of the "supernatural being" class, written in the "aged style" of "quiet heart and distant eye."

There are stands of bristlecone pine, *Pinus longaeva*, in the mountains at the western edge of the Great Basin that contain individual trees that are dated as more than four thousand years old. They are thought to be the oldest living beings.

Wovoka was the visionary founder of the Ghost Dance religion. He had a big hat that he sometimes let his followers peek inside: they said it contained all the wildlife and native homelands of the pre-white world.

Lord Krishna, when a baby, sometimes ate dirt. Once when his Mother tried to take a lump of dirt off his tongue, he playfully let her see the whole universe with its stars and planets, all in his mouth.

And a Zen story: When Huang-bo bid goodbye to Nan-ch'üan, who saw him off at the door, Nan-ch'üan held out Huang-bo's straw hat and said: "Your body is unusually big. Isn't your straw hat too small?" Huang-bo said "Although my hat is small the entire universe is in it."

Vimalakīrti was an enlightened Buddhist layman from north India who fell sick. In the sūtra named for him an incredible number of beings of all categories from all over the various universes come at the same time to pay him a sick call. No matter how many keep arriving, they all fit into his one small room, "ten feet square."

At various times over the recent periods of glacial advance there has been a vast inland sea, Lake Lahontan, covering much of the Great Basin. At the moment it is almost entirely dry.

By Way of Thanks

I thank the fellow writers who helped me shape this poem's idea from earliest on: Philip Whalen, Allen Ginsberg, Michael McClure, Jack Kerouac, and Lew Welch.

And my Dharma Teachers: Isshū Miura Rōshi, Sessō Oda Rōshi, and So(ko) Morinaga Rōshi. Nine bows.

Hosts of poets and writers, scientists, scholars, craftspersons, rivers-and-mountain people, fields-and-orchards people, and streets-and-buildings people have befriended and instructed this work. They are too numerous to thank by name. My gratitude to you all.

Thanks to the John Simon Guggenheim Foundation, the University of California at Davis (Research Grants), and the Foundation for Deep Ecology.

I am grateful for the readings and suggestions given the almost-finished manuscript by Peter Coyote, Alan Williamson, Scott McLean, Michael McClure, Jon Halper, David Padwa, and especially the witty and demanding Jim Dodge.

And thanks to Jack Shoemaker, friend of more than thirty years, advisor, publisher, and editor. I am indebted to his warmth, skill, and encouragement.

And finally, great thanks to my wife, lover, and partner, Carole Koda—at home in the world, at home at home, and a *dakini* of mountains and rivers.

Publication Record

The author wishes to thank those who have published sections of this work.

"Afloat": *Grand Street* 45 (Spring 1993)

"Arctic Midnight Twilight" published as "Daylight All Day": *Zyzzyva* 11:4 (Winter 1986–87)

"The Bear Mother": *Sulfur* 22 (Spring 1988)

"The Black-tailed Hare" published as "The Rabbit": *Poetry* 111:6 (March 1968)

"The Blue Sky": *Caterpillar* 5 (October 1968)

"Boat of a Million Years": *Wild Earth* (Spring 1996)

"Bubbs Creek Haircut": *Origin* 2 (July 1961)

"The Canyon Wren": Reprinted from *No Nature* with permission of Farrar, Straus & Giroux, North Point Press division

"The Circumambulation of Mt. Tamalpais": *Coyote's Journal* 5–6 (1966)

"Covers the Ground": *The Threepenny Review* 58 (Summer 1994)

"Cross-Legg'd": *Zyzzyva* 12:1 (Spring 1996)

"Earrings Dangling and Miles of Desert": *Yale Review* 80:1–2 (April 1992)

"Earth Verse": *Tree Rings* 9 (Spring 1996)

"The Elwha River": "Six Sections from *Mountains and Rivers Without End,*" *Writing* 9 (1965)

"Endless Streams and Mountains": *Orion* 14:3 (Summer 1995)

"Finding the Space in the Heart": *Shambhala Sun* (May 1996)

"The Flowing": *Kyoi-Kuksu* 3 (Spring 1974)

"Haida Gwai North Coast, Naikoon Beach": "Essays and Poems for Sherman Paul" in *The Green American Tradition,* (Baton Rouge: Louisiana State University Press, 1989)

"The Hump-backed Flute Player": *Coyote's Journal* 9 (1971)

"Instructions": *Sipapu* 50 25:2 (1995)

"Jackrabbit": *Sulfur* 22 (Spring 1988)

"Journeys": *Wild Dog* 17 (1965)

"Mā": *Coyote's Journal* 10 (1974)

"Macaques in the Sky": *Wild Earth* 1:4 (Winter 1991–92)

"The Market": *Origin* 12 (January 1964)

"The Mountain Spirit": *Sulfur* 39 (Spring 1996)

"New Moon Tongue": *Wild Earth* (forthcoming)

"Night Highway 99": *Origin* 4 (January 1962)

"Night Song of the Los Angeles Basin": *The Ten Directions* 7:1 (Spring–Summer 1986)

"An Offering for Tārā": *Yale Review* 83:1 (January 1995)

"Old Bones": "Essays in Celebration of Paul Shepard" in *The Company of Others,* ed. Max Oelschlager (Kivaki Press, 1995)

"Old Woodrat's Stinky House": *Yale Review* 84:3 (Summer 1996)

"Raven's Beak River": *Sulfur* 22 (Spring 1988)

"Three Worlds, Three Realms, Six Roads": *Poetry* 109:3 (December 1966)

"Under the Hills Near the Morava River": *Sulfur* 33 (Fall 1993)

"Walking the New York Bedrock": *Sulfur* 20 (Fall 1987)

"We Wash Our Bowls in This Water": *Yale Review* 84:3 (Summer 1996)

"With This Flesh" published as "Reeds": *Sulfur* 35 (Fall 1994)

Also by Gary Snyder

A Place in Space: Ethics, Aesthetics, and Watersheds

No Nature: New and Selected Poems

The Practice of the Wild

Left Out in the Rain: New Poems 1947–1985

Passage Through India

Axe Handles

The Real Work: Interviews and Talks 1964–1979

He Who Hunted Birds in His Father's Village

Turtle Island

Regarding Wave

Earth House Hold

The Back Country

Myths & Texts

Riprap and Cold Mountain Poems